EXMOOR WALKS

with **Rodney Legg**

whose circuits also appear

in **Exmoor – the Country Magazine** and **Somerset Magazine**

Wincanton Press

National School, North Street, Wincanton, Somerset BA9 9AT

For **Dr Philippa Woolf**
of Roadwater, who
helped me back to health

Publishing details
First published 1999. Copyright Rodney Legg © 1999.
Published by Wincanton Press, National School, North Street, Wincanton, Somerset BA9 9AT (01-963-32583) to whom updatings may be sent, addressed to the author. Distributed by Halsgrove, Lower Moor Way, Tiverton, Devon EX16 6SS (01-884-243-242).

Printing credits
Typeset in 10 on 13pt Weidemann by Julie Green with photographs by Rodney Legg. Printed in Somerset by F.W.B. Printing at Bennetts Mead, Southgate Road, Wincanton, Somerset BA9 9EB (01-963-33755).

Prints of Rodney Legg's photographs are available in 8 x 10 inch size (in colour or black-and-white depending on format of the original) at £18 each from Rocket Services, PO Box 342, Wareham, Dorset BH20 7HR.

International standard book number
ISBN 0-948699-70-1

Area Map

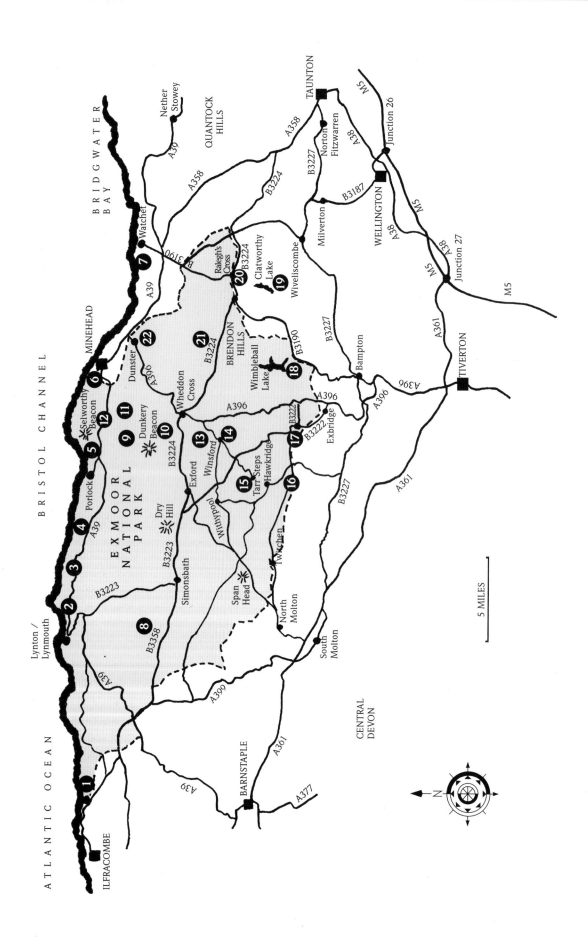

Introduction

ELEMENTAL IS the word for Exmoor. Climatically challenged is also a phrase that applies. Hill-fog, flash-floods, and brisk south-westerly winds; the problem is forecasting which and then coping accordingly. The situation for a visitor is not helped by the fact that its weather is often very different from the conditions one leaves behind in lowland Devon and Somerset. High, wet, and wild can be these uplands at their most magnificent.

Discovering Exmoor, for me, has been like visiting a foreign country. For a Dorsetman, who grew up beside the crystal clear waters of Purbeck and Lulworth, the initial culture shock of seeing the Somerset coast off Weston-super-Mare was to realise that cold greys worthy of the Kola peninsula and the approaches to Murmansk were the norm for the Bristol Channel. Steep Holm, on that December boat trip in 1973, looked like an austere rock that had been towed down from beyond the Arctic Circle.

Philip Watkins assured me that the Exmoor coast was something else. His advice was only put to the test after Jack Rayfield and Roy Smart hired me as their professional walker for Somerset Magazine, to research and tramp circuits along the lines of those I had been doing for years in Dorset.

The next stage in my education came when Hilary Binding and Stephen Pugsley established Exmoor – the Country Magazine … and sent me into the next county. That overdosed me with what I term sexy scenery. It performs to the highest international standards and is compellingly photogenic. Devon's seaside moors have an intensity of light and colour worthy of the Mediterranean and the Caribbean.

The bonus is a scattering of ancient burial mounds and standing stones as the occasional reference points in big country landscapes that are evocative and mysterious. Plus big birds and animals of the sort that are lacking in much of ordinary England. The red deer of the former Royal Forest of Exmoor, a mediaeval hunting ground, are truly a national treasure and represent our heritage as well as being natural history at its most magnificent.

Much of the best of Exmoor is in the care of the National Trust. The finest elements of Devon's coast are to be found on the Hangman Hills and the neighbouring 2,000-acre Lynmouth Estate, now extended eastwards at Kipscombe Farm and Countisbury Common, and the 12,479-acre Holnicote Estate boasts the most exquisite villages in Somerset, at Selworthy and Luccombe.

Most of the routes are along public rights-of-way but advantage is also taken of access land. Minimal road walking is sometimes necessary to complete a circuit; usually along quiet lanes that are attractive in their own right. Distances range between one and ten miles but Exmoor demands effort and energy that would take you twice as far in most of lowland Britain.

These are not military-style hikes. You will find some of the walks strenuous but many are suitable for the active elderly. Good walking, for me, is done at between one and two miles per hour, with frequent stops to observe vegetation and wildlife, to take photographs, and to take a closer look at anything half-way interesting noticed en route. Sometimes I move faster towards the finish, particularly as darkness forces the pace, but ideally leisure walking drifts and expands to fill the available time. Detours and diversions bring in any nearby ancient monuments.

All my walks are along public rights of way for preference, or across access land with freedom to roam, with permissive paths being utilised only where there is no suitable highway as the alternative. Permitted use is always subject to change and does not carry the same legal remedies for blockages, vegetation, or other difficulties. Neither are they usually shown on Ordnance Survey maps so us intruders are unaware of their existence. Even public highways can move, however, through a range of reasons from erosion to development, so you must always be prepared to adapt to the situation you find on the ground. The best I can ever do is describe paths as I find them. As chairman of the Open Spaces Society – Britain's oldest countryside pressure group, founded in 1865 – I have done my best through the 1990s to defend and extend the public path network.

The circuits are intended for individuals and those who enjoy a purposeful stroll with friends and family. On a personal note, group walking has always been anathema to me as it tends to take the fun and magic out of the experience; it is almost impossible to commune with nature if you are surrounded by a monstrous regiment of ramblers. One such straggle I encountered in the middle of nowhere and attempted to ambush by lying in the moor-grass, to photograph them approaching and then stopping beside Pinkworthy Pond, which was about the only landscape feature for miles. Surely, I thought, they would halt here. Instead, not a single anorak broke ranks, and hardly a head gave a sideways glance towards the shimmering waters. They might as well have been marching through the fenced corridors of urban alleyways.

Establishing a right-to-roam, turning the former royal forest into a people's moor, is going to be wasted on those who walk themselves into a coma and cannot appreciate the freedoms already there to be enjoyed.

Combe Martin and the Hangman Hills

EXMOOR ENDS in the west with clifftop moorland east of Combe Martin, where our walk begins with the Cornish-style bay and mini-harbour, from beside the Foc's'le Inn. We climb eastwards into Exmoor National Park and are treated to some of the finest blue-sea scenery of southern England. It is generally up to international standards in terms of colour and light.

Two miles of National Trust cliffs and moors follow, including the twin peaks of Little Hangman and Great Hangman (at 1,043 feet) and the expanse of Girt Down with Blackstone Point as an optional extra.

Some 500 acres are owned by the Trust around a core holding given in 1973 by Mrs T. Lethaby, as a living memorial to her husband, Major Lethaby. Look out for Peregrine falcons as well as our usual Exmoor companions, such as ravens and buzzards. The view across the Bristol Channel is to the Gower Peninsula. Hill farms follow

Cornish-style: Combe Martin Bay from Lester Cliff

and a series of droveways, across to Knap Down. Next are Silver Dale Nurseries, with tea gardens and the National Collection of Hardy Fuchsias. There is more Trust-owned land in the valley at West Challacombe. Throughout it is classic beauty on the western flank of Exmoor's holiday coast.

The limitations are that this is mostly strenuous terrain for a **six mile** circuit that can be extended to eight miles with optional diversions. There is a gruelling climb for a long two miles and then no refreshments en route until you return to Combe Martin. That said, there are few stiles or gates to

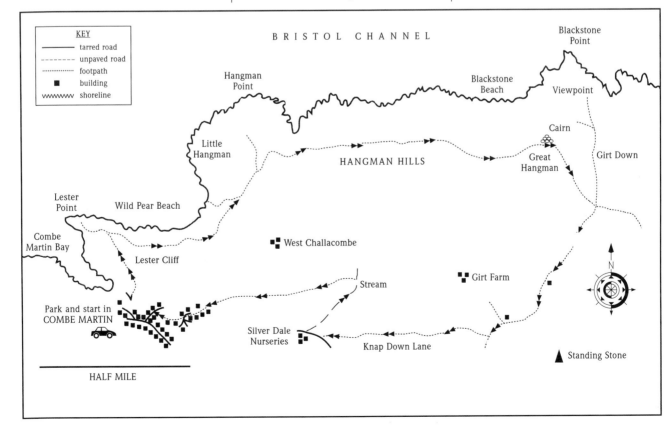

Far west: Exmoor begins here, as far as Devon goes, with a beach-pebble plinth

Nautical name: the walk starts from the Foc's'le Inn

contend with, and all the paths are well marked both on the ground and with signs. Expect damp patches below West Challacombe.

THE WALK ➤➤➤

APPROACH COMBE Martin on the A399 and turn from Borough Road into Cross Street, beside Sue's Newsagents. Park and start from the Kiln Car Park, which is beside and behind the Foc's'le Inn (Ordnance Survey map reference SS 578 474).

Set off northwards, from the top end of the car park where we take the path signed to Lester Cliff and the Hangman Hills, between the most westerly Exmoor National Park logo and Harbour Rise.

The path bends to the right, to the top end of the garden of Harbour Rise, and then forks right below the drive of Sea Closes.

A flight of steps beyond the gardens becomes an incline path up to the National Trust sign for Little Hangman, which is actually on Lester Cliff.

Here we have our first optional diversion, to continue straight ahead for the view over Combe Martin Bay from Lester Point.

Our walk, however, turns eastwards beside the sign, which is incongruously followed by what looks like a bus shelter, from which we admire Hangman Point. Expect to see Peregrines.

Keep following the coast path.

Our second optional diversion is down to Wild Pear Beach, romantically named and set in its own cove, using a zig-zagging smugglers' path.

Then we climb over the grassy foothills of Little Hangman.

Divert leftward and upward for a diversionary climb to the summit; a compelling if not compulsory diversion as it is a cop-out not to claim the summit. On a clear day, the Gower Peninsula is visible across the water – with Swansea, Port Talbot and Porthcawl to its right.

Our route, however, continues ahead and eastwards, following the stone wall to the bleak gorse-covered headland of Great Hangman in a mile.

From the cairn we proceed eastwards, towards a similar stone-pile on Holdstone Down, where unfenced common land allotments are partly Trust-owned. This path gradually bears right, south-eastwards, towards the inland valley.

On reaching the walled pasture at the edge of Girt Down we are faced with a crossroads of paths.

Turn left, northwards, for an optional diversion to the viewpoint on Blackstone Point, in half a mile.

Our circuit, however, turns the other way and we keep the pasture to our left. We are heading for

Above – Sandy Bay: the former inner haven of Combe Martin Bay

Right – Peregrine country: Little Hangman with Wild Pear Beach

Below – Between peaks: from Little Hangman to Great Hangman

Combe Martin and the road, south-westwards.

Leave National Trust land at the stile beside the gate and continue to proceed inland. The stone wall brings us to a barn and a farm road beyond the lambing pens.

The track is now a wide and stony green lane between stone walls.

Beyond Girt Down bungalow we continue straight ahead, with Girt Farm being down the private road to the right. To the left, a couple of fields away, is a substantial Bronze Age standing stone; upright and rectangular, about five feet high.

In 150 yards, just before the brow of the hill, we turn right into a narrower track which is signed to Combe Martin. This is Knap Down Lane.

In a kilometre we come to a tarred road and turn right along it, downhill.

Then turn right, in 100 yards, opposite the entrance to Silver Dale Nurseries and Tea Gardens.

Here our optional diversion, apart from the tea-room, is to see the National Collection of Hardy Fuchsias which thrive in these clement conditions.

Opposite the cattle-grid, our track is a semi-paved lane – again signed as a footpath to Combe Martin – which descends to West, North and East Challacombe. West

Challacombe, which is owned by the National Trust, is a neat 15th-century manor house and farmyard.

At the bottom of the hill we cross the stream and then turn left across a stile, to follow the waterside path through the ferny gorge.

After a footbridge the path then follows a lesser trickle, intimately at times, through a carpet of wild garlic.

It brings us to Challacombe House and a junction beside Silver Seas.

Here we turn right, following a sign to the beach via Hangman Path, and descend through a

narrow hollow way between the gardens.

Cross the stream beside Wayside and then turn left, along Rosea Bridge Lane, which is sandwiched between an ivy-clad Devon cob wall and the chain-link fence of the school.

Turn right along Borough Road.

Fork right after Sue's Newsagents, along Cross Street, which returns us to the Foc's'le Inn. ◆

Top – West Challacombe: most of the valley and its view are owned by the National Trust

Left – Standing stone: visible from Little Hangman, if you look south-east

Countisbury and Lynmouth

DEVON STARTS with woods and cliffs east of Lynmouth, which have the visual distinction of being the place where the Bristol Channel finally throws off its sickly brown-water overtones of tidal sedimentation and takes on a Mediterranean sparkle, or the clarity of Atlantic respectability. It is also just about solid National Trust ownership for three-quarters of this strenuous **five mile** route, along reasonably well-defined paths but expect loose stones in places.

We begin the circuit from the Exmoor Sandpiper at Countisbury and head southwards across Trilly Ridge into deep-cut woods of sessile oaks and the confluence of the aptly-named Hoar Oak Water with the East Lyn River at Watersmeet. Here, unusually for Exmoor, we have National Trust en route refreshments in Watersmeet House which was a quality Victorian hunting lodge.

Next are the first of the dramatic relics and reminders of the great flash-flood of 15th August 1952, which devastated the valley and its twin towns of Lynton and Lynmouth, killing and injuring dozens. The stumps of the washed-away crossing at Bridge Pool have been replaced by the smooth arch of Chiselcombe Bridge.

Between the oaks, the lush sessile oak woodland includes Devon whitebeam and mountain ash, with rare Irish spurge beneath, beside luxuriant ferns and mosses in the damper zones.

Our route follows the River Lyn through the towns to the quay and estuary, where as noted with pleasant surprise, the grey waters of the Bristol Channel give way to Mediterranean turquoise on merging with the Atlantic Ocean.

From here we turn east, to climb up and through the cliffside woods to re-enter National Trust land above Black Rocks and Sillery Sands. Defences on Wind Hill range from prehistoric Countisbury Castle to a cannon-site and its Second World War successor.

This is a stiff climb up steep slopes, though at least you are not having to push a lifeboat, from sea level to the 850-feet contour.

Next are clifftop Countisbury church and churchyard. In the latter rest most of the heroes, having reached decent old age, of the greatest feats in the annals of the lifeboat service which took place in 1899 when the Lynmouth boat was hauled across the high moors to Porlock in order to effect an epic rescue.

On returning to the Exmoor Sandpiper we are reminded that it used to be the Blue Ball Inn. It admits to having dropped its traditional name (at least it didn't become the Newt and Lettuce).

THE WALK ➤➤➤

Rocky gorge: the East Lyn on its way into Lynmouth

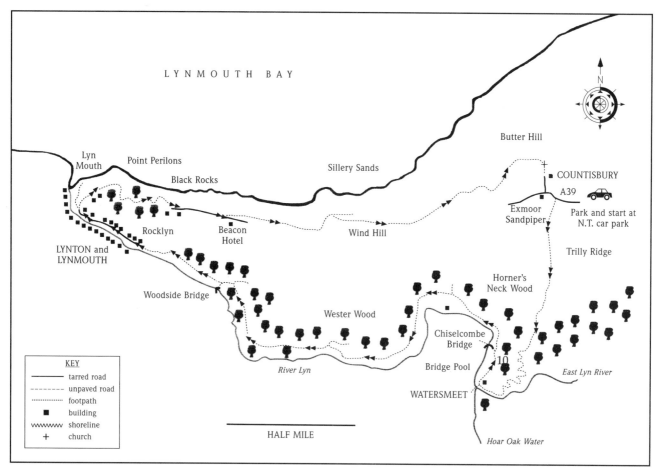

LYNMOUTH BAY

Butter Hill

Lyn Mouth
Point Perilons
Black Rocks
Sillery Sands
COUNTISBURY
A39
Park and start at N.T. car park
Exmoor Sandpiper
Rocklyn
Beacon Hotel
Wind Hill
Trilly Ridge
LYNTON and LYNMOUTH
Horner's Neck Wood
Woodside Bridge
Wester Wood
Chiselcombe Bridge
East Lyn River
River Lyn
Bridge Pool
WATERSMEET
Hoar Oak Water

KEY
— tarred road
--- unpaved road
···· footpath
■ building
wwwww shoreline
+ church

HALF MILE

APPROACH COUNTISBURY along the A39 to the Exmoor Sandpiper Inn which is midway between Lynmouth and County Gate. Park and start in the National Trust car park, which is on the north side of the main road, opposite the inn (Ordnance Survey map reference SS 747 497).

Set off eastwards, uphill along the main road.

Turn right in 100 yards, through the eastern of the two gates. We are now heading south, to Watersmeet, via Trilly Ridge.

At the end of the stone-walled track continue straight ahead, keeping the field wall to the left.

On reaching the gorse we bear slightly right to head for the tree-covered knoll in the middle distance. A sign points towards the gap in the scrub.

The path passes through the oaks of Horner's Neck Wood and patches of relict heather clumps on defunct anthills across the top of the knoll.

From here the track zig-zags down the steep wooded slopes towards the sound of Watersmeet.

Turn right at the path junction immediately above East Lynn River, as it approaches Hoar Oak Water.

Pass Watersmeet House, which was built by the Halliday family in 1830 as their fishing and shooting lodge. It is now the National Trust focal point for refreshments and information. Opposite the house is a mine adit, a horizontal shaft, cut in the 17th century to extract iron ore.

Keep on the east bank of the river after the confluence, bearing right along the track that rises above the water. Look down on Bridge Pool – here are the stumps of the ancient bridge washed away in the 1952 flood, upstream from the replacement stone arch.

Renamed roadhouse: the Exmoor Sandpiper used to be the Blue Ball Inn

This is Chiselcombe Bridge; bought by relief fund subscriptions and opened by Earl Fortescue in 1975. The charity tone to the inscription is something of an oddity in that these days one would expect weather-damaged highway bridges to be automatically restored at public expense.

From here there are options – to follow either the woodland or riverside paths downstream to Lynmouth. Our choice and recommendation is the former, because the river now turns westwards and its north bank, in the woods, has the best of both the sun and the views. That said, it also tends to be rougher under foot, as it passes below the scree slopes.

Keep going straight ahead at the past junction in Wester Wood. Our route becomes Arnold's Linhay. A plaque records that the snappily-titled Lynmouth, Lynton and District Association for the Preservation of Local Natural Beauty acquired the central valley for the National Trust in 1936.

Again continue straight ahead, westwards along the north bank of the river, after Woodside Bridge.

We arrive in Lynmouth beside the alluring Rocklyn Riverside Tea Garden above the restored river bank in the deep gorge.

Follow the river along the road and then follow the footpath

Above – Countisbury Castle: the stout rampart across Wind Hill
Below – Lyn Mouth: the quay and estuary, seen from the inspiringly named Eastern Beach

Hunting lodge: Watersmeet House now caters with National Trust refreshments

beyond Glenville House and Tregonwell Guest House (an intriguing connection with the 'founder' of Bournemouth).

The next section of road leads to the Manor Pleasure Grounds, to Rock House and the estuary, opposite the little harbour and quay.

Here we join the coastal footpath, turning right and eastwards, towards the Foreland and Foreland Point.

Turn right at the end of the promenade, along the coast path signed to Minehead. Lynmouth Bay is to the left with Point Perilous projecting.

In 20 yards we turn left and then left again at the next path junction, in order to zig-zag uphill through the woods. Keep going uphill, however inviting the alternative.

Join the A39 coast road opposite Countisbury Lodge and the car park for the Tors Hotel.

Turn left, uphill, along the raised pavement. The retaining wall, a project created to relieve unemployment, is dated 1925 and carries the name Hobbs.

We re-enter National Trust land opposite the Beacon Hotel and turn left into it, two yards beyond the Trust's 'Foreland' sign.

The coast path heads east, above Sillery Sands and Lynmouth Bay, with Port Talbot opposite.

Keep straight ahead, passing below a roadside viewpoint, and then crossing the site of a wartime gun emplacement.

Pass below the outer ramparts of Countisbury Castle outworks. The main Iron Age fortification is further inland on Wind Hill, with great banks across the promontory.

Beyond it the path kinks right and then left to follow the stone wall between the bracken and pastures. We are heading north-east along the coast path. On the skyline is a Coastguard lookout.

At the end of the walled pastures our walk leaves the long-distance coastal path. Turn right into Countisbury churchyard.

Here lie the majority of the crew of the lifeboat *Louisa,* which, in 1899 due to mountainous seas at Lynmouth, was hauled up Countisbury Hill, past this church and over the moor, to be launched ten miles away, down at Porlock Weir. Horses and men did the pulling, with bends on the narrow road having to be dug and widened in places, and in others the boat had to be lifted over obstacles. *Louisa* then went to the aid of the steamship *Forest Hall.*

Also note the tower pinnacles of the parish church of St John the Evangelist, which are dated 1836 and bear the initials of the churchwarden, R. W. S. Halliday.

From the churchyard, walk down to the gate, and follow the lane southwards to the car park and the Exmoor Sandpiper. Historically, our starting and finishing point was named the Blue Ball Inn, from 1800 to 1986. It then became the Blue Boar, just for one year, and has been the Sandpiper since 1987. ◆

Foreland Point: seen from a sea of rose-bay willow herb

Doone Country and Oare

WOOL-WEALTH, the clue to the proud towers of Somerset churches, has its least likely monuments in the most westerly coastal settlement in the county. Remote Oare parish embraces Exmoor at its most desolate. Beyond, across white-water rapids on the very edge of Devon, are the rubble ruins of the lost village of Badgworthy.

It is a landscape that demands have a book written about it. Fortunately, in the middle of nowhere, the grandson of a rector of Oare came across the magic and mystery of Doone Country.

The last inhabitants of the scenically idyllic oasis of green, beside streams at the heart of the central uplands, were the real-life Doones of legend before literature.

They were credited with brutal killings, in which age was no exemptor, as a doggerel verse implies:

'Child, if they ask who killed thee,
Say it was the Doones of Badgworthy.'

These brigands were stock-raiders and highway robbers, driven out of Scotland early in the 17th century, who found refuge in crumbling Badgworthy, and would eventually provoke the people of Exmoor into an uprising against them. The rest is literature, one might say, with Richard Doddridge Blackmore creating an alter ego to tell the story: 'If anybody cares to read a simple tale, told simply, I, John Ridd, of the parish of Oare, in the county of Somerset, yeoman and churchwarden, have seen and had a share in some doings of this neighbourhood, which I will try to set down in order, God preserving my life and memory.'

What unfolds is the story of *Lorna Doone, A Romance of Exmoor,* which with film and radio adaptations to introduce it to new generations, remains a best-selling classic. Its original appearance, as Blackmore's third novel in 1869, pioneered romantic fiction with a tragic heroine set in the context of solid historical research. 'Blackmore did for Devonshire' – and Somerset across Badgworthy Water – 'what Scott did for the Highlands,' says the *Dictionary of National Biography*, 'by conjuring up the romantic traditions and investing the story of old feuds and forays with his own imagination and fancy.'

It is now impossible to sift fiction from fact, with not only the Doone Country appearing on the Ordnance Survey map but also a

Lorna Doone Farm. The latter is some way from historic Badgworthy, with a monolithic memorial to R. D. Blackmore erected beside the path between them. Now it is the Doone Valley through which Badgworthy Water flows, down to its confluence with Oare Water after passing under Malmsmead Bridge.

All are in Devon, by a matter of yards, except for the mediaeval bridge, which straddles the county boundary. Somerset provides the eastern backdrop, and the setting for the goodies to ride to the rescue from Oare and beyond. John Ridd, the story-teller, lived at Plover's Barrow, on the hilltop above Oare House, in a farmstead that has now shrunk back into the wooded landscape.

As for the real history of Oare, of which Blackmore was aware as he had access to the parish records, it includes at least one instance of outlawry. Walter, the chaplain there, was murdered by Robert of Oare, in an incident which left the

Above – Embattled tower: wool-wealth church of Somerset's coastal extremity, at Oare

Left – First stream: Oare Water flows through Malmsmead

Left – Doone Country: its heartland, beside Badgworthy Water

Right – Village street: the track through mediaeval Badgworthy, home of the Doones

Below – Pullover time: the flock queues for a photo-call on Stowey Allotment

chaplain's son, Gervase, seriously wounded with sword cuts.

Oare, as a Domesday village of some significance, has a watery name in sound and fact, as it is directly derived from the Celtic name for its river, the 'Are'. This valley access was bridged in ancient times by Oare Bridge for the Oare Water, and Malmsmead Bridge across Badgworthy Water to the west, with both structures surviving as ancient monuments.

Eastwards, up stream towards Porlock, the valley route was and is tortuous with a carriageway that just about defies the name as it goes into ninety-degree bends either side of narrow Robber's Bridge. The road could well have been designed to trap the unwary, and then negotiates steep corners on its onward ascent through the woods.

Finding Oare can still be problematic, as its isolatory jingle implies:

'Culbone, Oare and Stoke Pero Parishes three, no parson'll go to,
Culbone, Oare and Stoke Pero, Three such places you'll seldom hear o'.

Not that this presents any difficulty with the parking and starting for setting out on this **ten mile** walk as there is an ample and conspicuous car park beside the A39 at County Gate, where Somerset meets Devon.

What is more important is to ensure that you are not lured into these high moors, which are as desolate as Exmoor can offer, during adverse weather. Wind and rain will be uncomfortable, painful even, but hill fog is a more insidious threat.

Following the valleys into the hills is the easy bit. What follows is a 1,350 feet featureless plateau. For some stretches there are walls to follow but these then come to an end and you are then on a compass bearing.

Map-using can be a hindrance rather than a help, and for reasons that Exmoor National Park Authority should have resolved decades ago. The legal line of the bridleway across authority-owned access land on Great Tom's Hill is 250 yards to the west of its signed route on the ground.

That's not a problem if you can see where you are going, but in dense fog when the clouds come down the line of the path on the map lures one to a point in a high stony bank with angled deer-fencing where there is no gate. One then has only a 50 per cent chance of turning the correct way in order to find the nearest opening.

In hill fog, yards can look and feel like miles, and with this sort of problem the compass now adds to your difficulties because to use it effectively you need to know where you are coming from. The problem, which applies to a mile of bridleway across potentially hostile terrain, should have been corrected by a formal diversion order to move the public path from its theoretical line on the map to the actual course on the land.

You have been warned – hill walking is at best strenuous and at worst can be positively dangerous. By all means rise to a challenge, but don't let bureaucracy compound the difficulties.

THE WALK ➤➤➤

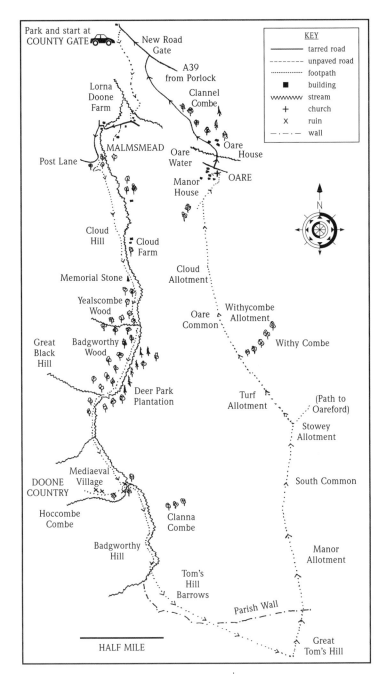

Park and start at COUNTY GATE

New Road Gate

A39 from Porlock

Clannel Combe

Lorna Doone Farm

MALMSMEAD

Post Lane

Oare House

Oare Water

OARE

Manor House

Cloud Hill

Cloud Farm

Memorial Stone

Cloud Allotment

Yealscombe Wood

Oare Common

Withycombe Allotment

Withy Combe

Great Black Hill

Badgworthy Wood

Deer Park Plantation

Turf Allotment

(Path to Oareford)

Stowey Allotment

DOONE COUNTRY

Mediaeval Village

South Common

Hoccombe Combe

Clanna Combe

Badgworthy Hill

Manor Allotment

Tom's Hill Barrows

Parish Wall

Great Tom's Hill

HALF MILE

KEY

——	tarred road
- - - -	unpaved road
········	footpath
■	building
∿∿∿∿	stream
+	church
×	ruin
—·—·—	wall

N

PARK AND start at County Gate Visitor Centre on the south side of the A39 on the Devon and Somerset boundary (Ordnance Survey map reference SS 793 486).

Viewpoint panorama panels, currently fading away, commemorate *Daily Telegraph* 'Country Talk' contributor John Peel who died in 1983.

Set off the other way, southwards through the gate opposite the Walkers' Shelter, along the grassy bridleway which follows the fence between the sheep pasture and the eastern wall of the car park. This is signed to Malmsmead and the Doone Valley. The main road is now behind us.

After following the stone-banked hedge the track becomes a downward terrace cut into the valley side. At the bottom it opens out into a wide double-hedged droveway.

Join another bridleway beside Oare Water and turn right and then left, over the footbridge, to walk up into the farmyard at Malmsmead.

Turn right along the lane, down to hump-backed Malmsmead Bridge, across to the Devonshire side of Badgworthy Water.

Here we turn left at the junction, beside Lorna Doone Farm, to follow Post Lane upstream.

In 350 yards, at the bend, we go through a field gate and follow a bridleway. This heads south, into the heart of Doone Country.

Cross the ford after the ash trees and then resume the southerly course, keeping the Doone Valley to your left. Its final buildings, at Cloud Farm and the Riding Stables are on the Somerset side of the water. You can cross the footbridge to the tearoom but then return to Devonshire to continue southwards.

Beyond the buildings the valley is deep-cut and makes the transition to a 'Beware of Brigands' landscape as we converge with the boulder-strewn white-water rapids.

Keep Badgworthy Water ('the cleanest river in the country,' I was assured) down to the left. We pass a memorial stone in 500 yards. The monolith, erected by the Lorna Doone Centenary Committee in 1969, has a slate to Richard Doddridge Blackmore whose novel 'extols to all the world the joys of Exmoor'.

There is also some evidence of 'real' history as we notice that the bridleway is an ancient road, still paved in parts with stone setts. Next we pass through the enchanted forest, more than a touch bewitched, of mossy and stunted oaks, in Yealscombe Wood and Badgworthy Wood.

Across the water, Deer Park Plantation is a very different tangle of impenetrable rhododendron and larch. Feel the humidity – even the water is now mossy – as ferns, liverworts and epithrites cling to every trunk and branch. This is said to be the dampest spot on Exmoor; the equal of Wistman's Wood on Dartmoor.

We then rise towards Badgworthy Lees and the bend in the river, where we cross a tributary that comes down from the west, off Great Black Hill.

Then in another 500 yards we cross a lesser brook off Badgworthy Lees.

In a further 600 yards another stream, plus path, joins from the west at Hoccombe Combe, beside the site of mediaeval Badgworthy,

on our side of the water in Devon. This must be one of the most remote lost villages in England.

Divert up the track for 250 yards, to walk the grassy street and see the best of the ruins, being a two-roomed farmstead with stone walled paddocks each side.

Then descend to the confluence of the Hoccombe stream and Badgworthy Water.

From here we proceed south-eastwards, towards Exford. Continue to follow the main river, Badgworthy Water, which resumes a southerly course, to a footbridge in a kilometre.

Here we turn left, across the river, and then set off into the high moors, south-south-east towards Exford. We are back in Somerset, passing Tom's Hill Barrows – natural mounds rather than man-made – and climbing Great Tom's Hill.

Keep the stone wall, which is also Oare parish boundary, across to your right. Our path gradually converges with it and goes through a gate.

Bear left on the other side, heading south-east for 750 yards.

Here we join a bridleway, beside the fence, and turn left along it. We are now heading north and re-cross the wall in 400 yards. This is where the gate and pointers are – confusingly, the Ordnance Survey shows the legal course of the path some way to the west, where there are no holes in the wall.

Our course is now north-north-east, towards Oare, across Manor Allotment.

Keep straight ahead after going through the fence into South Common, to cross Stowey Allotment, at 1,350 feet above sea level. Don't expect to see any cultivation, let alone a Brussels sprout, for these are sheep pastures.

Here we bear left, towards Oare rather than Oareford. We are heading north-west, towards County Gate which may be faintly visible on an overlapping skyline.

Keep straight on once more, beside Turf Allotment (still wild, across the bank to our left).

In 700 yards, above Withy Combe, we go through the left-hand of the two gates, into Turf Allotment, with Withycombe Allotment now being the pasture across the fence and bank to our right. We are heading towards Oare Common and Cloud Allotment, both now sheep pastures, in half a mile.

Stay on the west side of the bank, keeping it to our right. Proceed straight ahead through the gate 15 yards to the left of the next corner of Cloud Allotment, in 300 yards.

We are heading north and bear left to begin the descent into Oare, where Oare House is the first roof to appear beneath scrubby Clannel Combe.

Go through the gate to its left, between Oare House and the almost-skyline County Gate buildings.

From the lower end of this pasture we head towards chimneys on our side of the valley. Go through the gate and descend to Oare parish church, which is dedicated to St Mary. The Manor House is to the left and we emerge on the road to the right of both the church and manorial outbuildings.

Turn left on reaching the road and visit the church, which also has its Blackmore memorial, this time complete with bearded caricature.

Turn right at the junction. Cross Oare Water at mediaeval Oare Bridge and follow the lane uphill to the main road, at New Road Gate. One of its stone posts is still in situ.

Turn left at the junction, walking westwards towards oncoming traffic, to county Gate in a straight and survivable 400 yards. ◆

Above – Fictional fact: this is Lorna Doone Farm, beside Malmsmead Bridge

Below – Bearded author: the memorial to Richard Doddridge Blackmore, doing its bit for church funds at Oare

Culbone and Worthy Combe

EXQUISITE CULBONE, deep in the woods on Exmoor's coastal slope, claims to be 'the smallest complete church in England'. It is also almost unique as a place out of bounds to motor vehicles, where the only access is on foot.

The dedication is a further rarity, being to Saint Beuno, a monastery founder from Clodoch in the Black Mountains who was laid to rest on Bardsey – 'the Isle of the Saints' – in about 623 AD. There was a tiny community at Culbone in Saxon times, but then it was known as 'Cyta-Ore' for 'cave by the sea', which became corrupted as Kitnor in the Middle Ages.

Then its isolation brought refugees and outcasts. They created an 'enclosure' in about 1265 and were followed by a prison colony from 1385 to 1450.

There followed a leper settlement from 1544 until 1622.

The miniature church has a leper-squint window on the north side of the nave, permitting them to watch services from outside in the churchyard.

Finally, the valley became home to 38 prisoners of war, captured in 1720 whilst fighting for the French in India, and they remained for 21 years. Some stayed longer, working as charcoal burners and bark-strippers in the cliff-hanging woods, producing the raw materials for leather tanning.

The churchyard became virtually a private burying ground for members of the Red family, the oldest being John Red who died in 1832 and the most recent headstone being to Irving and Ethel Red who both died in 1966.

The handful of other names include James Court of Ashley Combe: 'For more than sixty years woodman and faithful friend to the first and second Earls of Lovelace and to Mary Countess of Lovelace.'

Measurements are part of the Culbone story. The church has a chancel 13 feet 6 inches long by 10 feet wide, opening into a nave 21 feet 6 inches long by 12 feet 4 inches across. The walls are two feet thick.

There is a 13th-century sandstone chancel arch and a matching Norman font. An anchorite's cell in the north side of the chancel has a two-light window, carved from a single block of faded red sandstone, which is two feet wide and has the outline of a primitive head incised on the outside at the top, between the two arched slits.

Porlock panorama: from a horethorn tree to the Bristol Channel

Topping off the roof is a dainty spire, added in 1810 and said to be the former top of Porlock church spire, which was blown down in a storm. Beneath are two small bells, including a 'long waisted' early 14th-century specimen which is the oldest bell in west Somerset.

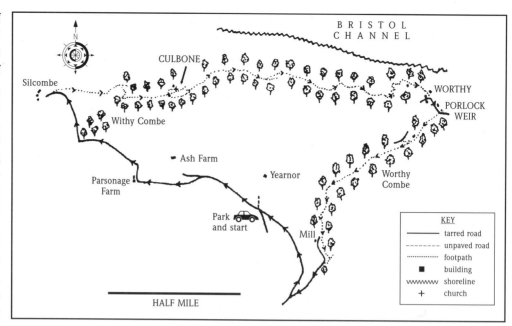

Others have enthused over Culbone – notably Sir Nikolaus Pevsner, who described the 'utter solitude' as 'delightful, with the rushing stream, the screen of wooded hillside and the distant corner of the sea. Equally delightful is its own shape and surface, with the little slate spire riding on the nave roof, and the whitewash having come off in irregular patches to expose rubble stone underneath.'

Culbone is the primary objective of this **five mile** walk which also explores another pleasant but motorised glen at Worthy Combe on the return circuit to your vehicle.

En route in the car you have a chance to stop by the road and stroll into a ragged wood of stunted pines to see a reddish two foot high standing stone. The Culbone Stone, which is close to the parish boundary, is carved with an incised wheeled cross which is a ballot-paper type 'X' set in a circle of four-and-three-eighths-inches diameter.

This has been claimed as a 6th-century Christian carving but it

Superlative claim: 'the smallest complete church in England' is at Culbone

might pre-date that and be a Celtic cartwheel motif. The evidence for this is that the 'X' in the circle has an outward line extending from the bottom right which was added later, apparently to 'Christianise' a pagan stone. The extended incision is less deep than the design inside the circle and twice the width of the other lines.

Either way, it is a romantic stone in a wild place.

THE WALK ⟩⟩⟩

TURN NORTH off the A39 Porlock to Lynmouth road opposite Culbone Stables Inn, which is three miles west from the cattle-grid on the summit of Porlock Hill. After turning off the main road you cross another cattle-grid and then pass a layby with a short waymarked path to the Culbone Stone.

The walk begins a mile further down this road, from a crossroads with signs to Porlock Weir, Silcombe Farm, Yarner Farm and Ash Farm (Ordnance Survey map reference SS 848 476). There is parking for a couple of cars on the grass to the right but if this space is taken then you have to go back up the hill for 700 yards to the grass area on the right, 100 yards downhill from your third cattle-grid and the woods, and walk back down.

Turn left at the crossroads, along the road that is signed 'Alternative Path and Ash Farm'. It goes uphill and then downhill. Keep on the tarmac and pass above Ash Farm in half a mile.

Next is Parsonage Farm, where the road bends to the right at a catalpa tree and goes left and uphill, above Withy Combe woods and its stream. From here you climb again, with a panoramic view of the South Wales coast, and in 400 yards you approach Silcombe Farm.

Turn right as it comes into sight, along the path signed 'Culbone ¹/₂, Porlock Weir 2¹/₂'. There are

Celtic claim: a pagan cartwheel appears to have been converted into a Christian cross

warning signs of 'unstable ground between Culbone Church and Worthy. Risk of sudden, unexpected landslides.' You descend to a gate and the track reaches the woods.

Here we turn abruptly right, following a red marker on to a second path, stony and narrower, that drops down into the trees. It then follows a stream and brings you to a house in 200 yards.

Fork right on approaching its main arch, to pass under a second ivy-clad arch beside a waterfall. In 50 yards you reach Culbone churchyard with its lines of headstones to the Red family of Broomstreet.

After seeing the church you leave the churchyard by another gate, just beneath the spire. Then turn left and go left again on reaching the house, following the 'Coast Path, Porlock Weir' sign.

This points you over the arched bridge and you go left again on the other side, along a path which carries a further safety warning of 'unstable ground' and potential landslips. This path was perfectly walkable at the time we researched the walk but in the event of new problems you must turn back and retrace your steps along the official 'Alternative Route' which is the path you have already walked, back to your car.

Above – Landslipped cliffs: be prepared for diversions on the coastal path
Below – Curving walls: thatched pay-gate for the Worthy Combe toll road

Hopefully, the path is open and usable for the length of these delightful woods, which are a mixture of species including sweet chestnut, mountain ash and even the occasional strawberry tree amongst the sessile oaks. The roar of the sea replaces the babble of the stream.

For the first half mile you gradually climb along a terraced

path. Then it forks left and slopes the other way, in a descent of a further half mile.

Keep on this main track which is signed to 'Porlock Weir'. It zig-zags left and then right on the last leg, via steps and then under arches beneath a fort-like folly.

You reach the tarred road at a semi-circular thatched toll-house, which is the pay-gate for the

'Worthy Combe Toll Road'. Turn left, and then go straight ahead, away from the gate.

In a hundred yards, just before Worthy Manor, you turn right up a wooded 'Alternative Path' which is also signed as the 'Bridleway to Yearnor Mill Bridge'.

This ascends Worthy Combe, following the stream for half a mile. Keep following the blue bridleway arrows. There is a road to your right, on the other side of the stream.

A hundred yards after Yearnor Mill you come to the edge of the wood. Turn right here, at the fence-line, towards 'Culbone'.

Then in 50 yards the track bends to the right and bridges the stream.

Turn left at the tarred road and walk uphill for 250 yards. You come to a junction and turn sharp right, uphill towards 'Countisbury 7, Lynmouth $8^{1}/_{2}$'.

In 700 yards you reach the crossroads from where the walk started. ◆

Bossington and Hurlstone Point

Final turf: the last grass on the Holnicote Estate, before the moor reaches the sea

WORDS ARE superfluous when it comes to introducing a bracing walk on the rugged and romantic corner of the Holnicote Estate where Exmoor drops into the sea. Visual experiences abound throughout this **four mile** walk, upwards from the delightfully picturesque village of Bossington, along well marked paths that penetrate the open moor and coastal heights.

The intimate views are over Selworthy Sand and the tree tops towards Allerford. The great western panorama is into Devon, to the silhouettes of Old Barrow and Foreland Point where moorland vegetation gives way to that of the Atlantic seaboard. As does the bird-life, with circling buzzards and croaking ravens, then jackdaws and razorbills on the cliffs. Deer slots are there to be noticed, if not the beasts themselves.

This evocative landscape is the coastal sector of the 12,443 acre Holnicote group of holdings which were given to the National Trust by Sir Richard Acland in 1944. It comprises a collection of Exmoor gems and about the only ordinary scenery, appropriately, is the valley through which the main road approaches, between Minehead and Porlock.

THE WALK ➤➤➤

TURN NORTH from the A39 at Allerford, passing the famous packhorse bridge, or alternatively from the eastern end of Porlock. Head for 'Bossington 1'. Park in the village at the National Trust car park, the entrance to which is between Wayside, Kitnors, and the Orchard guest house (Ordnance Survey map reference SS 898 480).

Next to this is the 'Bridleway to Hurlstone Point'. Cross the river at North Bridge and turn left, along the track to 'Hurlstone 1'.

This follows the river for a short stretch downstream and then forks right, upwards along the side of Bossington Hill. After the chalet you descend towards the sea but then fork right, through a gate, to climb through open ground beside Hurlstone Combe. Look down on the bank of pebbles to your left. These cover the mouth of Horner Water. In flash floods 'it burst up through the pebbles with a tremendous roar', to quote a National Trust information panel.

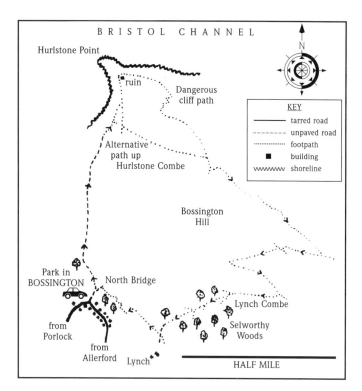

BRISTOL CHANNEL

KEY
— tarred road
--- unpaved road
···· footpath
■ building
wwww shoreline

Hurlstone Point
ruin
Dangerous cliff path
Alternative path up Hurlstone Combe
Bossington Hill
Park in BOSSINGTON
North Bridge
Lynch Combe
Selworthy Woods
from Porlock
from Allerford
Lynch

HALF MILE

Around you the vegetation grows wilder. The hollyhocks of the cottage gardens give way to greater mullein and foxgloves. Further up, on the windward slopes above the scree, are expanses of heather moorland and dwarf gorse.

At the National Trust's 'Hurlstone' omega-sign – ominously placed beside an emergency Coastguard telephone – you are given two options. We shall take heed of the warning but for now you proceed straight ahead to the gaunt shell of the former Coastguard Station on Hurlstone Point.

On reaching the second warning sign ('Dangerous Path beyond Coastguard Station') you turn on to the alternative path, if you are being cautious – take your choice.

Either way it is worth going on the Point to see the Victorian stone blockhouse that is the old Coastguard lookout. Around it the headland is smothered with thrift and a miniature species of stonecrop.

North Bridge: a ford takes the old road to the sea into the woods

From here, if you decide to stick with the potentially 'Dangerous' coastal option, you cross the stile and keep to the path along the exposed slopes. Then turn right, still following the dirt track as it zig-zags inland up the northern lip of Hurlstone Combe.

On the other hand, if you chose the safer alternative route, you turn left inland and walk up the middle of Hurlstone Combe, along the strip of grass between the bracken.

The two paths meet again at the top of the Combe, which is half a mile south-east of the Coastguard Station.

Here you keep your back to the sea and take the 'Coast Path' uphill towards 'Minehead' (and then

Coastguard Station: now roofless, on Hurlstone Point

'North Hill' which confusingly appears on another sign). Away to your right is the cairn at 800 feet on Bossington Hill.

As you continue inland you cross and ascend a great tract of open moor. In half a mile, at the next pointer, we turn sharply right and head towards the inner cove of Porlock Bay.

You are now walking downhill passing a long embankment which seems to be associated with Second World War defences or training targets. An underground bunker at its opposite end has been sealed with concrete.

Fifty yards after the fortification mound you pass a path junction at a yellow marker post. Then turn left, on to another path, beside another marker in 15 yards. This second path goes out on to a bracken-clad spur as you head towards the fields between Porlock town and Porlock Bay.

On the outcrop, at another yellow marker post, the path bends abruptly leftward, to face the side of a wood on the opposite slopes of a deep-cut valley. As you turn you look down on the hamlet of Lynch, with its 16th-century chapel incorporated into the main

barn of a later farmyard, at Park Farm

As you reach the valley floor, at a seat in Lynch Combe, take the first turning right. This heads towards the wood. Cross a little stream and follow the rocky path through the outer belt of trees.

Lynch Chapel: 16th-century stones as an adjunct to farmyard thatch

Left – The Street: Bossington is a fantasia of flowers and foliage

Below – Picture postcard: chocolate box perfection, with hollyhocks and thatch in Bossington village

Keep the wall of the main wood to your left and ignore the paths into it. Yours is that for Lynch which follows the outer wall, down the valley.

Also ignore a second gate, to your left, and likewise another to your right. The main track continues downhill, now between two walls, to a five-barred gate beside a field.

Here you leave Selworthy Woods, at a National Trust sign.

Turn right in 50 yards, into a field. Pass the site of a sheep-dip and walk along the lynchet that gives Lynch its name. Admire two walnut trees.

Immediately upon entering the next field the path turns left, to 'Bossington'. Follow the fence downhill for 50 yards, to a hunting gate in the corner, beside a holly bush.

Descend to the oak tree, in five yards, and turn right after the three steps below it. You are now walking above the river, which you can hear and glimpse to your left.

On going through a kissing gate you turn left and cross the river at a ford and footbridge in 45 yards.

The gate on the other side is into the National Trust car park. ◆

Minehead Harbour and Burgundy Chapel

Lone artist: Minehead is the St. Ives of Somerset

MUCH OF the heavily wooded corner of the Exmoor coast between Minehead and the National Trust's Holnicote Estate is also in public ownership. Greenaleigh Point and its cliff pastures were acquired by the Trust in 1985 and the extensive wilderness woods of Culver Cliff and Moor Wood are owned by the Exmoor National Park Authority.

There is no problem finding a circuit of suitable paths for this **four mile** walk from Minehead Harbour, or rather there is – for just that reason. This is one of those rare places where there are sometimes too many paths, not so much being too much of a good thing, but defying concise description.

I was tempted to opt for a permissive path up these overgrown and landslipped gullies in that a National Trust invitation to 'follow the footpath down the cliff slope' from North Hill to Burgundy Chapel made it sound an easy alternative. In trying it in reverse I found it was an exercise in damage limitation as I contended with brambles, rocks, and slime across a gushing springline.

Therefore our excursion to the chapel is along a flatter westward approach that is the sensible person's access – and then back the same way to rejoin our circuit at Greenaleigh Farm. It is a worthwhile diversion and worthy objective, being one of those evocative and mysterious places that exist for no obvious reason.

Not much is left of an early mediaeval domestic building, perhaps a hermitage, on a narrow platform between the cliff, the stream, and the sea. Immediately east of it is another rectangle of sandstone rubble, about 13 feet wide by 30 feet long, with a finely-carved doorway in its single standing wall.

This is a later mediaeval chapel, dedicated to the Holy Trinity, which has been attributed to an otherwise unknown member of the Luttrell family in thanks for his safe return from the Burgundian War, in the 14th century. That's hardly required history any longer, which I drink to, and I have taken the date from the sign beside the chapel.

In fact the main conflicts in Burgundy were a little later, after 1404, when John the Fearless joined the English invaders and conspired in the assassination of the Duke of Orleans, and would himself be assassinated at Montereau, in 1419. That was during the period in which England won the battles but lost the war, being evicted from all of France except Calais (and its supermarkets) by 1450.

Minehead's other treasure that is en route, behind protective glass, is the beautiful gothic script Missal of Richard Fitzjames. He was the town's vicar, who went on to be Bishop of London, from 1506 to his death in 1522. The volume of handwritten masses and sacraments pre-dates him by several decades; it returned to

Classic view: church to the left of the familiar profile of seaward Minehead

Minehead, via Sotheby's salesrooms, in 1949.

The principal clue to its dating, pre-1350, is that St Anne's Day is featured in red lettering – showing it dates from before the Kalendar reform that reduced her in status to a black letter day.

The Minehead Missal is in St Michael's Church which is the town's major cliffside landmark, towards the top of Higher Town with a tower that almost reaches the woods. It overlooks a delightful cottage quarter that is a village in character and as much as an anachronism as Minehead Harbour when it is deep in silt and left dry by the receding tide.

Minehead not only has one of the most 'strikingly situated' churches in the land, to paraphrase its guide, but that harbour, about which I am so disparaging, was its contemporary as one of the premier seaports of the West Country. Visually and historically it has its parallel in the famous Cobb at Lyme Regis. Both still retain their

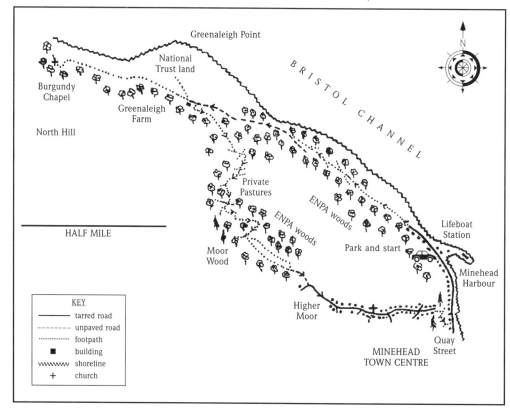

KEY

——————	tarred road
- - - - - -	unpaved road
....	footpath
■	building
wwwww	shoreline
+	church

lifeboats and notice boards listing the latest exploits of the guardians of our holiday coast. Hopefully you will not need search or rescue services, but take care not to stray from our route into the wilder uplands beyond. Take a straight line in most directions and it is five miles to the next habitation. So keep to the path.

THE WALK ➤➤➤

PARK IN the northern part of Minehead seafront, on or beside the promenade or close to Minehead Harbour (Ordnance Survey map reference SS 971 471). Our walk starts from here. If you have parked closer to the town centre then set off northwards along Quay Street – with the sea to your right – to the marvellously named Old Ship Aground, where you then pass the Lifeboat Station and continue for the length of Quay West.

The last house is Sea Crest, offering accommodation and a tea-room, after which you join a 'Public Bridleway to Greenaleigh Farm'. This path starts from the telegraph pole immediately beyond Sea Crest and follows a track at the bottom extremity of the woods, above the beach-side lawns.

Keep on this main track which continues straight ahead, uphill, for half a mile. You are climbing through the sycamore trees, rhododendrons and foxgloves of Culver Cliff Wood. Loud upward croaks will be from the ravens – the great black birds that command the stone pines. 'There are more of them here than at the Tower of London,' a fellow walker told me. 'They breed very early in the year and soon there are the young as well.'

To your right is the Bristol Channel, with South Wales and its power stations on the other side, and the twin 'Holmes' – Flat Holm and Steep Holm – are upstream, in mid-water.

Our path becomes an untarred road. On reaching the first pastures beyond the trees, above and beyond Culver Cliff Sand – you enter National Trust land, overlooking Greenaleigh Point.

The unpaved road brings you to Greenaleigh Farm, a mile into our walk. Here we continue straight ahead for 'Paths to Burgundy Chapel and Beach'. Immediately after the farm we continue ahead along the terrace signed for 'Burgundy Chapel (remains of)'.

This is a cul-de-sac path to one of Somerset's remotest romantic ruins, in half a mile, on the far side of deep-cut and landslipped Burgundy Chapel Combe.

From here we have to retrace our steps to Greenaleigh Farm and continue for just 50 yards beyond it.

Turn right, uphill and inland, on to a sunken trackway through the trees that is signed to 'North Hill'.

Continue straight ahead at a minor crossroads of woodland tracks, and then do the same at a more conspicuous one, with a seat: 'Rest Awhile – Happy Memories of Colin and Mary Cozens.'

Turn right at the next junction of tracks, uphill. Then fork left at the following offering of paths, still taking the uphill option. We are now approaching a hilly pasture, to the left, across which you can see Minehead Bay, its expanse of drained marshes, and the coast beyond Blue Anchor.

Our walk starts to descend, through birch woodland, to a crossroads of tracks to the right of a cattle-grid and blue-painted gate. This leads into the far corner of the hill pasture – which is private and has no public access. 'North Hill' is signed to the right. Make sure that you have found this point, before proceeding further, as it is one of the few landmark locations in hundreds of acres of identical landscape.

Now continue straight ahead, along neither of the afore-mentioned alternative paths, but into what is signed as the 'Woodland Walk'. This heads downhill and bends to the left, through the sweet chestnuts of Moor Wood. The public path is along its southern edge but signs indicate that we can use the main forest track, which descends via a zig-zag as you head south-eastwards, towards the Higher

Beyond Butlin's: end of the line for the West Somerset Railway, which shows up clearly from the hills

Left – Romantic ruin: the doorway of Burgundy Chapel opens on to Exmoor's coastal woodlands

Centre – Clockless striking: Jack Hammer's mechanism, in the parish church at Minehead, is mentioned in churchwardens' accounts for 1641

Bottom – Vehicle-resistant: cobbles, cottages and thatch along the ascent to St. Michael's Church

Town district of Minehead. Continue for 500 yards.

On the far side of Moor Wood you come to a narrow pasture with woods on either side of it. Face towards your glimpse of the Quantock Hills, with the railway line heading towards them in the middle distance.

According to the map there is a public bridleway along the left side of this wedge of grassland. On the ground, however, we are lured on to an alternative permissive path which is just inside the right-hand wooded slope. Its stile is beside a gate.

Either way we arrive at the same point as the two paths converge on the far side of the pasture, in 350 yards, and from here you continue straight ahead, down this dirt road, for a further 200 yards.

Turn left on emerging at the tarred road, away from Higher Moor. At the next corner we fork left, after Somerset Riding Centre and Hillside Barn. You are now in St Michael's Road, above Moor Road's round-chimney thatch at Lower Moor Cottage.

Head for the parish church. Its tower and the sloping churchyard are perched on a high red wall, above the picturesque cobbles and thatch of Church Steps and its cottages. Church treasures are the exquisite 17th-century bell-ringer, Jack Hammer – no longer at his clock – and the illuminated mediaeval manuscript that was the Missal of Richard Fitzjames. Its thousand pages contain the lifetime's scribings of more than one monk.

Follow the main road around to the left of The Cross and The Ball, to pass Marston Lodge Hotel. Next is the war memorial.

Here we can continue straight ahead, into the cul-de-sac beside the post box. This is Weirfield Road.

At the end, to the right of the drive to Green Gables a footpath continues straight ahead. We come to a junction of paths at the top of the wooded cliffs.

Turn right here and then left in another 50 yards, for the final drop through the cliff pines. Turn left at the bottom, beside a sign for the South-West Peninsula Coast Path which encourages you to set off for Land's End and Poole Harbour.

Our path is less ambitious, being about to emerge on the promenade beside the thatch of Seagate Cottage. You are back in Quay Street. ◆

Washford Station and Warren Bay

THE SCENIC face of industrial archaeology accompanies this **five mile** circuit of public footpaths between Exmoor and its coast. The route is from Washford to Old Cleeve and along the rough and rugged cliff top west of Watchet, from Chapel Cleeve to Warren Bay.

For more than a mile we walk beside the steam trains of the West Somerset Railway, with a bonus in the form of the path itself, plus the Somerset and Dorset Railway Museum and its collection of rolling stock and signal boxes at Washford Station.

One of the boxes is from Burnham-on-Sea and the other is fitted out in imitation of that at Midford. 'Except that the door is in the wrong place,' and a host of other points too technical for me to understand, inflicted on us ordinary decent visitors by a railway purist who insisted on coming between the punters and their imaginations.

Our later path beside the railway, back into Washford, has what can be the constant mewing of buzzards. Here the only other user for that mile and more was a single silent cyclist. It is a low causeway which formed the track-bed of the narrow gauge West Somerset Mineral Railway.

This was built in 1858 to bring iron ore from Victorian mines in the Brendon Hills, down to Roadwater and Washford, and then along the section which is now a public path.

It then went on to West Quay at Watchet Harbour. From here the ore was shipped across the Bristol Channel to the foundries of Ebbw Vale. One wonders what they do there these days – having not heard of the place since Michael Foot was its MP and writing of his famed predecessor Aneurin Bevan. Though there are still plenty of

Orchid cliffs: above the alabaster veins at Warren Bay

chimneys making a dirty yellow-brown haze along the South Wales seaboard, so some residual industrialisation must continue.

Wales looks distant enough from the Exmoor coast to appear as another country, where they probably do things differently, and the approaches to the hill-country of western Somerset are now overrun by the leisure trade.

Its two railways, past and present, run in parallel. The broad gauge branch line, which would be incorporated into the Great

Western Railway, arrived at Watchet in 1862. Its extension from there to Washford and Minehead was completed in 1874.

Conversion from Brunel's pioneering wide gauge to the ordinary and much more restrictive 4 feet $8^1/_2$ inches – it meant smaller and less stable carriages – took place on the weekend of 29th October 1892.

The following century saw the demise of extractive industries and commercial shipping, and their replacement by caravans and

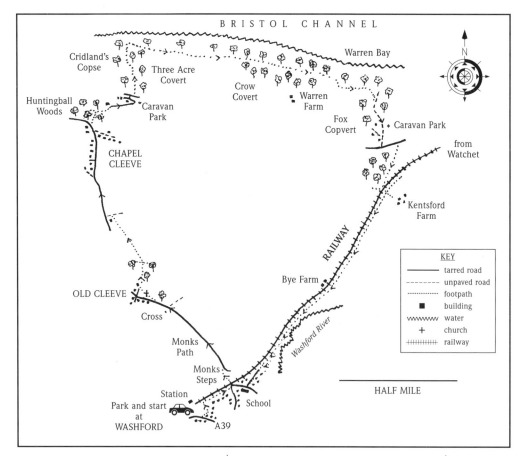

KEY
- ———— tarred road
- - - - - - unpaved road
- ·········· footpath
- ■ building
- wwwww water
- + church
- ++++++++ railway

HALF MILE

As well as the railwayana, there is plenty of traditional history on and beside the route, and a colourful geology. The 'celebrated alabaster rocks' – veined with alabaster and gypsum – are exposed along the coast from Cleeve Bay to Watchet. Offshore, coming out of the water at low tide, are the remains of a submerged forest.

The paths are all easily found and unobstructed. Many are more or less flat and there are no serious slopes to contend with. The lush vegetation, however, can be another matter, and it would be sensible to bring your secateurs.

camping. The latter would quite literally save the line, in the form of handouts from Sir Billy Butlin's holiday park at Minehead, when Dr Richard Beeching's axeing of rural lines led to the closure of the Taunton branch by British Railways. That happened on 4th January 1971 and was set to have been followed by the removal of track and the breaking of the bridges.

Instead, the new West Somerset Railway was born, and after overcoming a series of setbacks succeeded in reopening the line, on 28th March 1976. It has since brought back a succession of historic locomotives, some for period stays and others as guest visitors, to operate what is now Britain's longest steam line in regular seasonal service.

You are advised to keep to the paths set out at Huntingball Woods, including a section of permissive path north of the Beeches Holiday Park, because the coastal footpath further west has been closed. Our route keeps you on quiet wooded paths; whereas the alternative marked diversion on the ground is along a third of a mile of potentially unpleasant main road.

THE WALK ➤➤➤

PARK AND start from Washford Station, which is beside the Washford Inn and the A39 at the west end of the village (Ordnance Survey map reference ST 044 412). The Somerset and Dorset Railway Museum includes a signal box and equipment made to look like that at Midford (apparently only the 'Up Inner Home' at plate 14 is actually from there) and train tablet apparatus from Bath Junction.

After visiting the railway exhibition and discussing the parking arrangements – at busy

Heavy metal: ex-British Railways locomotive 44422 glistening as she backs along the bank into Washford

times you may be asked to leave the vehicle elsewhere – we turn left along the A39 and pass Washford Inn and its car park.

Then turn instantly left, to walk the length of the left-hand wall, with house No. 62 to your right.

In 50 yards we turn sharp left and follow the footpath sign for the Old Mineral Line and Watchet. This path is sandwiched between back gardens and the railway line. Turn left on reaching the road junction.

Go under the railway bridge and then ascend the Monks Steps. These join Monks Path which is the narrow road up and over the hill into Old Cleeve, in half a mile. On the hilltop we pass the stump of a mediaeval wayside cross.

Drop down into Old Cleeve and turn right on entering the village, following the footpath sign to Blue Anchor which takes you through St Andrew's churchyard. Here there is a much more impressive preaching cross, plus the ancient parish chest in the porch, which is cobbled with beach pebbles.

Exit from the opposite corner of the churchyard to that through which you entered it. Here we descend the steps and then proceed straight ahead, into an overgrown double-hedged trackway.

This crosses a sunken section of ancient road, with a flight of steps through the red earth on each side. The public path enters an arable field and heads left of centre, diagonally across it. Leave the field by crossing the stile near the corner, between the house and the field gate.

Turn right on reaching the road and follow it uphill for a third of a mile, into Cleeve Chapel, to the public path at the lower end of the Huntingball Woods.

Turn right here, up a public footpath, which turns right to pass to

Above – Railway Museum: the West Somerset Railway is the refuge for relics of the closed Somerset and Dorset line
Below – Train tablet: the machine that once controlled the line at Bath Junction

the right of the house and then continues up its drive. The top end of the path is a tarred road into the Beeches Holiday Park where it swings to the left and then right to drop to the B3191. Cross the road.

Turn right and then left, in 30 yards, along a permissive path, courtesy Crown Forestry, which replaces a public right of way that has been lost to coast erosion. We are walking through Three Acre Covert and Cridland's Copse. The track weaves through scrub and hart's tongue fern to the coastal footpath.

Turn right along it, east towards Watchet. As you get a sea view, with Steep Holm prominent in mid-Channel, Weston-super-Mare emerges to the right of it and south Wales stretches out to the left. Blue Anchor, Minehead and Exmoor are behind you – so remember to turn around for one of the classic Somerset views, from Dunkery to the sea.

We follow the cliff path for a mile, to beyond Crow Covert with its contorted ash tree, and Warren Farm. Look out for a glimpse through the leaves of the seaward end of Watchet Harbour, protruding from behind the headland. The path crosses a stile into a field and then turns left, into and across the next field. You are again heading back into the woods, with a diversionary path to the left if you wish to go down to the beach.

Our route re-enters the scrubs and emerges on a concrete road. Turn right, away from the sea, and walk up through the wood, which conceals Warren Bay caravan park.

Turn left along the main road, which is the B3191, for 150 yards. Just around the corner, after the caravan sign, we turn right through a field gate.

This hillside incline is signed 'Old Mineral Line', and gives a perfect view of the West Somerset Railway which emerges from beneath St Decuman's Church and Watchet Paper Mills, into a long valley beside Kentsford Farm.

Here we 'Stop Look Listen' – hopefully having to wait for steam – and then walk across the line.

Turn right at the crossroads of paths on the other side and follow the track-bed of the former mineral line to Washford, in a mile. All the way we are close to the standard gauge railway, on the other side of the trees to our right. To the left are the tall masts of a Government Communications Headquarters listening post, spying for Cheltenham.

Bye Farm is to the right in half a mile. Next is the Washford River which leads into Lower Washford.

Here we turn right, beside Old Cleeve First School, and walk along the road to the railway bridge.

Beside it, straight ahead, is the public path which returns us to Washford Station. ◆

Steaming west: the line to Minehead, passing Kentsford Farm

Pinkworthy Pond and the Saddle Stone

Industrial project: John Knight's embankment dammed the headwaters of the Barle, in 1830

THIS IS a pilgrimage to the far north-western corner of Somerset, high and bleak in the heart of Exmoor, where you look north to Lynton beside the Bristol Channel and west to Barnstaple and the Atlantic Ocean.

It has been virtually uninhabited since prehistoric man came down from the hills. Conveniently for us the Bronze Age peoples left the few distinctive landmarks in these parts, such as the outsized Woodbarrow which stands far above the present tree-line. Further west the Longstone Barrow is also in view though the Long Stone itself – a slender nine feet in height – is just over the horizon. Likewise the skyline Chapman Barrows and their standing stones but mediaeval Somerset can answer back with the Saddle Stone and Edgerley Stone.

These markers, with the Woodbarrow midway between, delineated the extremity both of Somerset county and Exmoor Forest. Hereabouts there is little else apart from the occasional antiquity in a vast open landscape of purple moor grass, cotton grass, bog asphodel and deer sedge. There is more of the latter on The Chains than anywhere else in southern England.

In fact this and the adjoining look-alike moors comprise one of the biggest wilderness areas south of Yorkshire. Nearly 2,000 acres, including the first part of our **five mile** walk, were formerly part of the Pinkworthy Estate which was purchased by Somerset County Council in 1969 and handed to the National Park Authority.

Its focal point is Pinkworthy Pond. This was the creation of Midlands ironmaster John Knight, who had bought much of western Exmoor in 1819, and devised a scheme in 1830 to harness the headwaters of the River Barle. He also built two canal-like leats towards Simonsbath, and seems to have planned industrial developments there, but they and the project failed to hold water.

His legacy is the deep-water reservoir of Pinkworthy Pond, where the red deer drink in summer – for the rest of the year there is water just about everywhere. It oozes from each tussock and makes this a walk where sensible footwear is an imperative. Ditto warm clothing and a map and compass. For when hill-fog and the clouds descend – which at 1,600 feet they can do for a pastime – one clump of deer sedge, or even a beautiful heath spotted orchid, looks much like another.

You then have to find a wall and follow it in the required direction until you reach a valley road. In extremis you'll feel as if you are competing for the Duke of Edinburgh's award; be warned that Exmoor rain is colder and wetter than the benign sort that falls in your garden. Viz the Lynton flood disaster, of which more en route.

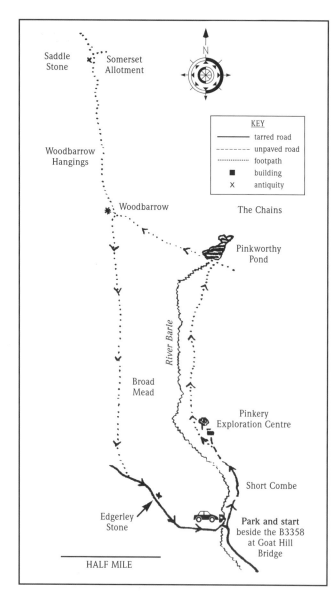

KEY
——	tarred road
- - -	unpaved road
········	footpath
■	building
x	antiquity

HALF MILE

Boundary marker: the Saddle Stone props up Saddle Gate, at the extremity of western Somerset

Therefore you should only hit these hills after a favourable weather forecast. Better still, listen out for the Lundy shipping forecast. You need light winds (force 5 or below), no rain, and good visibility. The shipping forecast is the highest grade information going and absolutely relevant. Going up into the hills is much like venturing out to sea.

It covers a 24-hour period, so it is ideal for decisive last-minute decision making. If in doubt – don't.

THE WALK ➣➣➣

TURN WESTWARDS from the B3223 on the west side of Simonsbath, along the B3358 which is signed for Challacombe and Ilfracombe. Park and start in

three miles, from beside the stone wall on the north side of the wide bend at Goat Hill Bridge (Ordnance Survey map reference SS 724 406).

Go through the gate beside the access road to Pinkery Centre for Outdoor Education, on the east side of the River Barle. This track is signed: 'Footpath only to Pinkworthy Pond 1½. No cars.'

It passes through Short Combe Rocks and then approaches the Exploration Centre.

Fork left, across the pasture, to skirt the left-hand edge of the shelter belt. These are the first and last trees you will see on this walk.

After the wood the footpath bends to the right and passes through an old stone bank.

Turn left of centre in this next pasture, to head northwards, towards The Chains. Keep the river to your left and go through a gate in the beech-hedged wall that pens

the open moor. Yellow pegs and the occasional boardwalk and stepping stones mark our path, above the eastern bank of the Barle.

Soon our first major objective is in view, being the embankment across the top of the valley, which is the dam retaining the cold waters of Pinkworthy Pond.

Go through the gate and then turn left, across the top of the embankment, along the path signed to Woodbarrow in half a mile. The path follows the fenced bank and then goes through another gate, to leave National Park Authority land.

Head right of centre across this next section of spongy upland. Woodbarrow emerges on the north-western skyline. To see this large Bronze Age burial mound we momentarily step into Devon.

Northwards from here, also through the gate, we head across the great plateau – a little left of centre – following the Barbrook sign.

Our next objective is a kilometre away on the almost empty skyline, to

Added graffiti: showing that the historic Edgerley Stone can almost be called accessible

Exploration centre: formerly Pinkery Farm, with the highest wood in west Somerset

the right of the glimpses of the distant Lynton and Lynmouth coast. It is damp ground up here at 1,566 feet; indeed this was the epicentre of Britain's most disastrous localised rainfall of the century, on 15th August 1952, when one Exmoor gauge recorded nine inches but upwards of eleven inches must have fallen here within that fateful 24 hours. That's a sixth of the year's rainfall in a day.

Torrential flooding converged on Lynmouth and Lynton, where two deep-cut valleys funnelled the raging waters and washed away bridges, roads and houses.

To the left, as you cross the high moors towards Lynton, are Woodbarrow Hangings, with the Longstone Barrow at the top of these short, sharp valleys.

Gradually our view of the lower Bristol Channel opens out, as we begin to drop down to Thornworthy Common.

Go through Saddle Gate at the junction of the two stone walls. The bench-marked Saddle Stone stands six-feet high, set in the bank beside the gate – having once been its post.

We now follow the right-hand fence down to the next gate, in thirty yards. Turn right, through it, into Somerset Allotment. The stones beside the long west to east fence, to your left, mark the county boundary with Devon and the extremity of the Royal Forest of Exmoor.

The corner of the fence appears to be at the precise north-west corner of Somerset, though it is somewhat confusing as the wire otherwise fails to follow the legal line; abandoning an acre of the county to Devon's Thornworthy Common.

From this romantic and isolated spot we have to turn around and retrace our steps – after a fashion – southwards to Woodbarrow.

Here we continue south – straight ahead through the gate – to the B3358 in a mile. The track follows a bank, to our right, but legally we are in the next county as Somerset lies unmarked a few yards to our left. Spiritually this is definitely Devon, being on the Tarka Trail that celebrates author and otter-lover Henry Williamson whose Braunton Burrows landscape is visible beside the western seaboard.

It seems strange to find oneself walking across Jeremy Thorpe's old constituency. Particularly for me, as this late-life discovery of the Exmoor coast was stimulated by one of his acolytes, Philip Watkins, then the national treasurer of the Liberal Party.

The path follows a secondary fence to the left as it approaches the main road. Exit across the stile beside the gates.

Turn left, uphill, and walk on the right-hand side towards oncoming traffic.

After the first bend we re-enter Somerset, with the ancient Edgerley Stone (much like the Saddle Stone) being set in the left-hand bank.

In 500 yards, after the next couple of bends, you are back at your car. ◆

Isolated landmark: Woodbarrow, dating from the Bronze Age, is on the Devon border

Pinkworthy Pond: Somerset's highest lake, at 1,500 feet elevation, surrounded by The Chains

Stoke Pero and Horner Wood

SOMERSET'S NEWEST national nature reserve covers 4,000 acres of central Exmoor. It was created by English Nature on 18th October 1995 and extends across the county's highest moors at Dunkery, merging into the adjoining commons, and dropping into the deep-cut wooded valleys around the northern foothills. All of it is dramatic scenery, forming the upland core of the Holnicote Estate which Sir Richard Acland gave to the National Trust in 1944.

The huge nature reserve surrounds a block of isolated hill farms, between Stoke Pero and Cloutsham, which are also Trust-owned and crossed by bridleways which complete the circuit for this **six mile** walk. Its ancient gem is the mediaeval church of the otherwise lost village of Stoke Pero. Stoke where? There is a rhyme to that effect:

*'Culbone, Oare and Stoke Pero
Three such places you'll seldom
hear of . . .'*

High moor: the habitat above the tree-line, on Stoke Pero Common

You are certainly far more likely to see red deer than local residents and this part of what is now Luccombe parish is off the usual visitor trail. That there is still a church rather than a ruin is due to the rebuilding of 1897, at the expense of lord of the manor Sir Thomas Acland, in celebration of Queen Victoria's diamond jubilee. The hero of the work, displayed on a sketch hanging in the nave, was Zulu the donkey who plodded twice a day for months to bring all the timber for the replacement roof, from sea level at Porlock. It was calculated that he hauled the loaded cart a total of 1,000 miles (plus the same empty) and up a combined height of 22,500 feet.

It is the highest church in Somerset but even so it stands on a platform cut into the hill and is well short of the summit which rises from 1,013 feet at Stoke Pero to 1,704 on the top of the county at Dunkery Beacon. That was also the high point of the old parish until it was absorbed into Luccombe in 1933.

'Together we must have more pew space per head of population than anywhere else in the land,' I was told at Luccombe. 'The sad thing is that it is only properly used these days when we have another funeral.'

Other hill farms have disappeared in their entirety. Prickslade and Bagley are now empty names. Likewise the tenement cottage at Stoke Bridge, where our walk makes its western turn – north to Pool Bridge and Horner Water – fell into ruin and was remembered for the outline of its garden and a single surviving cherry tree.

Horner Water must be one of the best trout streams in the West Country. Its interest for English Nature, leading to the creation of the Dunkery and Horner Wood National Nature Reserve, is that its

High farm: Wilmersham sits on the hill above Stoke Wood

gorge-like shelter and high humidity have endowed it with the best lichen collection in the British Isles.

The species list is now well above 200 with all four of the rare Lobarion types being present. Many occur on dead wood, which is left to decay, and fungi, liverworts and extreme rarities such as the Filmy Fern also thrive. The red deer herds help by congregating here, using the remote woods as their traditional harbourage, and keep the woodland floor grazed at just the right level of the eclectic botany.

As for bird life, pied flycatcher and wood warblers breed here. The

sessile oaks do not grow to any great size but form a dense canopy and form what is in parts a genuine primaeval woodland. *Usnea florida* is the lichen sprouting from them.

Above, in the transitional zone between these damp lowlands and the exposed upland habitats, is the largest national stronghold of the rare Heath Fritillary butterfly. It is also the best area for sighting buzzards and ravens, both individually and in occasional quantity, mewing and croaking as they gather in families from the tree-line below.

Also look out for merlin – as much chance here as anywhere in Britain – curlew, ring ouzel, and the introduced red grouse. Underfoot, both sides of the tree-line, the general groundcover is whortleberry or bilberry as we know it in the supermarket. The moors are a mixture of that and

bell-heather, with bristle bend grass in the open areas and western gorse for the scrub-belt.

It is excellent but strenuous walking country – six miles up and down the high moors requires the time and effort of twice that in normal countryside. Beware too of look-alike scenery. Following a field hedge with a view over the Bristol Channel to the industry of South Wales lulls one into a deceptively good sense of location that is suddenly lost on entering the woods where all trees, streams, rocks and even offshoot valleys are utterly identical. They are so deep-cut that you also lose contact with the direction of the sun and paths that seem the follow the compass on the map in fact meander and wind in gross contortions.

That is a caution I'll reiterate at a strategic moment in the text – but try and keep it in mind throughout. Also watch your feet as well as struggling to see a sky-line, given that the condition of the paths is a direct extension of the rapidly changing landform geology – and therefore liable to change at any moment from rough and stony to something better described as a scree-slope.

Take care, as this is just the sort of terrain where you can twist an ankle. It is also a landscape that can soon become climatically-

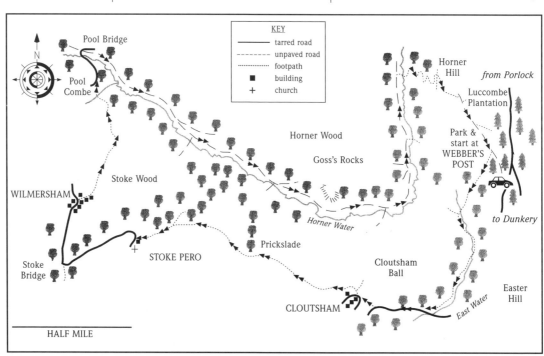

White water: rocks and rapids in Horner Water, running through the National Nature Reserve

park. There is a current lack of signs – causing a number of lost souls for me to direct and round-up – but this path appears to be part of the nature trail and heads towards the hamlet of Horner.

It goes through the pines to a stone seat, commemorating the Acland family and their donation of this vast estate to the National Trust. In a further 120 yards, after the seat, you turn sharp left, down through the gorse, along a path signed 'Priestway Stoke Pero'.

Keep straight on along this path and ignore the right-hand turns. In the wood we turn left, upstream, and then cross the footbridge.

Continue along the track beside the stream and ignore another on the right which is signed to Stoke Pero. Our path will get you there, but via the picturesque and rocky valley into Cloutsham. This is East Water.

Follow the white-water rapids upstream for half a mile. On joining the tarred road we turn right, away from the ford and towards Dunkery.

Continue along the road for 400 yards, to the bends, and then fork right, up a stony track. This ancient public road climbs to the farm, which was built by the Aclands in the style of a Swiss chalet.

Immediately after emerging on the sharp turn beside the buildings we turn right along another stony track. This one is just about flat and leads northwards into the fields. It is signed for the nature trail, but instead, in 50 yards, we follow the

challenged, with anything from a blizzard to hill-fog when it disappears into the cloud, so listen for a forecast before you depart.

THE WALK ➤➤➤

PARK AND start in the main car park of Dunkery and Horner Wood National Nature Reserve. This is situated beside the pines at Webber's Post which lies inside the cattle-grid of the high moor, a mile

south-west of Luccombe village. Approaching it from the Porlock direction, coming south via Chapel Cross, you fork right (towards Cloutsham and Exford) upon rising on to the plateau above Luccombe Plantation. Then turn right, in 125 yards, into the western section of the car park (Ordnance Survey map reference SS 904 437).

Set off northwards, following the main track into the pine trees from the middle of this part of the car stone walled cul-de-sac around to the left, towards Stoke Pero.

Then go through the field gate and turn left. Follow the hedgerow to the end of the field. Then follow the fence straight ahead, above Prickslade, into a sunken trackway leading to the southern edge of Stoke Wood, beyond which we enter a dark tunnel of double-banked leafy lane.

The farmstead in the light at the end of this tunnel is just about all that remains of the former village and parish of Stoke Pero. Beyond Church Farmhouse you will have a real treat.

'I will lift up mine eyes unto the hills,' to quote Psalm 121. St Peter's church, at 1,013 feet above sea level, is Exmoor's highest and most isolated. It was restored in 1958 and includes memorabilia and photographs celebrating its famed inaccessibility, which was complete from Boxing Day until April during the 'Great Winter' of 1962-63.

From here we turn right, downhill, and follow the road westwards into and through Wilmersham Wood. There is a steep descent to Stoke Bridge and a similar gradient to climb on the other side.

In 500 yards the road brings us out of the wood and up to Wilmersham Farm.

Fork right immediately after the last roadside barn and descend along a farm road between more barns. Then walk along the track beside the front wall of Wilmersham Cottages.

After the buildings the bridleway takes the left-hand of the two field gates that are in front of you – into a sunken green lane. Continue straight ahead along this track, north-eastwards through three gates.

Immediately after the third the bridleway turns right, downhill across the field, and enters the Pool Combe arm of Horner Wood. slightly left of centre, in the dip, there is a gate into the trees.

Turn left in the wood and go down to the ford. After crossing it the track turns right and climbs to a tarred road in 150 yards.

Turn right, downhill, to the loud and lively Horner Water. Cross the stone-arch Pool Bridge and turn

Sheep fleece: wind-blown wool in St. Peter's churchyard at Stoke Pero

right, following the river downstream, south-eastwards for more than two miles, almost to Horner.

You'll soon find that all the trees, rocks and rapids look identical, so start counting the footbridges. Ignore the first, which is in a mile, and likewise the second, in a further half mile.

In another half mile the river and track bend to the left after a clearing, following our passage below Goss's Rocks which were tree-covered above and to the left.

Pass the third bridge – which is also hidden in the trees and easy to miss. We also ignore another track which is signed for Cloutsham and Dunkery Beacon.

Look out for the next right-hand offshoot, in 500 yards. This bridge is clearly visible, on three stone piers, with five steps down to the path on the other side. Cross it and count the steps, just to make sure.

From here we go straight ahead, for twenty-five yards, and then turn left, along a hillside path signed to Webber's Post. Walk it with care as it zig-zags uphill, across an active scree-slope.

Halfway up the hill we turn right and then left, in just ten yards. Tucker's Path, this overgrown section of the nature trail is called. We are heading generally eastwards, and upwards, towards Webber's Post.

On the summit, some 600 yards from the footbridge – though it will feel longer – we come to a dirt road. Turn right along it, south-east, to pass the Acland commemorative seat and return in 600 yards to Tucker's Path, it is called, and you turn right at the summit, along a dirt road back to the Acland commemorative seat and the car park amid the pines. They reminded me of Bournemouth and my native heath. ◆

Dunkery Beacon and the Top of Somerset

Somerset's summit: the cairn on Dunkery Beacon touches 1,704 feet, with nature working hard to reduce it

DUNKERY BEACON is the superlative Somerset peak, rising from the heather-clad roof of Exmoor. When you ascend its 1,704-feet summit you are standing on the highest hill in the county. To be pedantic about the exercise, it entails clambering up the conical-shaped cairn.

Even that, however, does not mean you are at the highest point in Somerset. For that accolade must go to the HTV transmitter on the Mendip Hills, the top of which touches 2,001 feet.

Dunkery rewards with a view that bridges the Bristol Channel, to Wales, is flanked eastwards by the Quantock and Brendon Hills, and extends south across the uplands of Somerset and Devon to the next

National Park, which is Dartmoor.

County historian John Collinson wrote of Dunkery as 'a very large and high mountain, standing in the several parishes of Cutcombe, Luccombe, Wootton Courtenay, Stoke Pero and Exford. Its base is about twelve miles in circumference.'

It was and is a hill of sheep and red deer that was an inspiration for poets of the romantic movement. In the process it tended to grow in stature. Collinson, through to *Kelly's 1889 Directory* – and writers who have copied them – had no doubt that it was 'the highest mountain in the western counties'.

These days the aviation chart – which has to be the final arbiter of

altitude – gives that prize firmly to Dartmoor with 2,038 feet at High Willhays.

Which is not to belittle our Exmoor summit. The stones on top of Dunkery were once 'three large fire-hearths' that comprised its beacon, 'in order to alarm the country in times of civil discord or foreign invasion'.

It stood a fair chance of being seen, unless Dunkery's head was in the clouds: 'When the air is clear and serene the line which bounds the horizon cannot be less than 500 miles in circumference, and takes in 15 counties.'

Some of the beacon stones were reconstructed, with cement, into the present main cairn. Built in 1935, this commemorates the gift of the summit and the surrounding moor to the National Trust.

The plaque puts the name of Sir Thomas Acland first among the benefactors but in fact 'Dunkery Beacon and 800 acres of land round' were the gift to the nation of Lieutenant-Colonel Walter Wiggin in 1932, when he was Master of the Devon and Somerset Stag Hounds.

Earlier Exmoor history lies beneath a series of Bronze Age cairns or round barrows that are the hilltop burial mounds of prehistory. They are pimples on an otherwise featureless horizon. Most are scheduled ancient monuments and the collection scattered across Trust-owned land in the vicinity of Dunkery include Great Rowbarrow, Little Rowbarrow, Kit Barrows and Joaney How Cairns. Robin How is close by but I failed to spot it.

This **five mile** walk brings in the Beacon high-point and some of the antiquities, in a circuit that is almost entirely on National Trust land.

For a complete contrast it also includes a couple of the magical deep-cut wooded glens where streams tumble off the moor. Some of the herd of Exmoor's famous red deer are generally present in the second part of the walk and buzzards circle outwards from the oak woods.

THE WALK ➤➤➤

TURN SOUTH of the A39 between Williton and Minehead, onto the A396 which is signed to Dunster and Tiverton. In seven miles, on the hills beyond Dunster, you come to the Rest and be Thankful Inn at Wheddon Cross.

Turn west here, on to the B3224. This is the Exford road and it is signed to Dunkery.

In seven-tenths of a mile you come to a corner at Blagdon Close. Turn right here, into a narrow lane signposted 'Dunkery 1½, Luccombe 5'.

Omega sign: Exmoor north from here to the coast is in the care of the National Trust

You cross a cattle-grid and a bridge in a mile and a half. Immediately beside the River Avill there are two parking areas. This is Dunkery Gate and the walk starts from the National Trust's 'Dunkery' sign, set in stones on the left-hand side of the road (Ordnance Survey map reference SS 896 406).

Beside it, to the left of the stone, a track goes straight ahead, uphill. Continue on the same path at the finger post in 200 yards, along the track signed 'Exford 4'.

In half a mile there is a junction with another track,

beside the point where the left-hand field hedge makes a 90 degree turn to the left.

Here you turn sharply right. You are now heading towards the conical cairn on the summit of Dunkery, in another half a mile. Pick up a stone to add to the loose cairn.

A topograph helps with your bearings. We have come from the

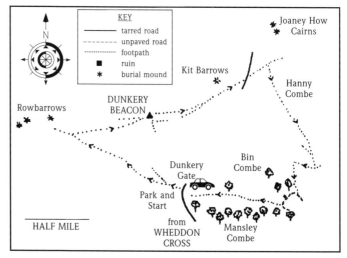

Riding by: huntsmen emerging from the tree-line, coming out of Mansley Combe

track that runs parallel to the 1,674-feet twin peak of Rowbarrow. Further away, on the Welsh side of the Bristol Channel, are Porthcawl (22 miles), Nash Point (16 miles), the Sugarloaf Mountain (52 miles) and Barry (21 miles). Mid-Channel are the islands of Flat Holm (24 miles) and Steep Holm (23 miles). 'Weston-super-Mare 27½' is an impossibility; it is blocked by the National Trust's headland of Brean Down.

Another piece of National Trust Somerset is Brent Knoll (27½ miles). Most conspicuous of all is Hinkley Point nuclear power station (20 miles). Inland, the line of the Quantock Hills becomes

obscured by the Brendon Hills and then the flat tops of a great land-mass on which you may be lucky enough to pick out Yes Tor from the rest of Dartmoor (37 miles).

Nearer at hand, you head towards the pinpoint for 'Weston-super-Mare'. This track extends left of centre towards Bridgwater Bay, which is the sea off Watchet. The path, which is rocky, descends gradually north-eastwards, whilst keeping to the spine of the ridge.

In half a mile it rejoins the main track and you continue straight ahead, passing Kit Barrows which are to your left.

In another half mile you come to the tarred road. Cross to the other

side and continue downhill. Two of the skyline burial mounds of Joaney How Cairns are prominent to your left. Keep your eye on them.

As they begin to vanish from view, in about 250 yards, you turn right. A lesser track goes through the heather above the lip of Hanny Combe. The sea and the wide green valley of the River Avill are now to your left and unbroken heather to the right.

A mile of gradual descent, keeping in a straight line south-eastwards, brings us to the edge of the moor and the chequer-board of neat fields around Wheddon Cross.

Do not leave the moor. Instead you turn right and keep the field bank immediately to your left. Ignore the next gate, in a 100 yards, and follow the once-layered beech hedgerow at the top of the highest pasture of Ford Farm. This former hedge is now as high as a house.

In another 200 yards we follow the hedge to the left as it turns at 90 degrees and goes downhill. Towards the bottom of the slope you pass into rhododendron scrub and leave the moor at an 'ENP' gate, initialled for Exmoor National Park.

Near the bottom we come to a farm road and turn right along it. You pass a ruined barn to your right and in another 50 yards the track fords the stream which drops over the mossy rocks from Bin Combe.

On the other side you fork right, uphill, with a bracken-covered slope rising to the right and the trees of Mansley Combe down to your left. Near the top of the slope you go through a gate.

Then turn left of centre, uphill, to pass to the left of a tall line of beech trees, in 100 yards. They are set on an old hedge bank.

After the trees you go slightly right of centre, continuing gradually uphill. After crossing a little brook this path bends to the left and becomes a stony cart track.

In a quarter of a mile it brings you to a gate and then to your car, at Dunkery Gate. ◆

Looking down: from the top of Somerset, on users of the topograph on Dunkery Beacon

Luccombe and Wootton Courtenay

PICTURE POSTCARD Luccombe is at the heart of Exmoor. It is one of the villages of the Holnicote Estate, given to the National Trust by Sir Richard Acland in 1944, with Somerset's highest open moorland rising to the south of Dunkery Beacon. Ditto, to the north-east, the estate hamlet of Tivington, where a time-warp combination of thatched cottage and chapel was given to the National Trust in 1997, to keep it in regular use.

The third settlement on this reasonably demanding **seven mile** walk, is the 'ordinary' village of Wootton Courtenay, also picturesque in itself but beyond the Trust's boundaries.

Of old Luccombe, at the time it came into Trust ownership, we know an immense amount, through the happy coincidence that it was selected for an intimate survey by wartime Mass-Observation, which became the basis of the book *Exmoor Village* by W. J. Turner.

It even gives the tenants' view of their last private landlord, Sir Richard Acland, who emerges as a complex and confused character. 'Isn't he a Liberal or something?' one woman asks. 'He was Socialist, you know' says an informed visitor. 'He'd got no time for gentry or the like o' they.'

Sir Richard shared their confusion and stood for Parliament in the 1945 general election, unsuccessfully, under the banner of his own self-styled Common Wealth Party. Eyebrows must have been raised when Robert Forgan, fascist deputy to Sir Oswald Mosley, addressed a meeting for him.

As for the life of the village, the book contains diagrams showing facilities at Luccombe and in the surrounding countryside. In the Second World War it had a church, letter-box, parish council, school,

Tower turret: final flourish at Luccombe parish church

shop, telephone kiosk, and village hall. Villagers had to travel between two and four miles for their baker, butcher, chemist, doctor, grocer, ironmonger, post office, policeman and public house.

The next tier of offerings, between four and six miles, provided a cinema, draper, hospital, passenger railway station, and secondary school. More than six miles away were the goods station, infirmary, and petty sessional court.

It is a list of bandings that is still largely correct, though in this

Exmoor is the exception rather than the norm, given that in most places just about all categories would have moved into the next as a result of the age of mobility.

'The villagers' thoughts run on animals,' Turner writes. 'Hunting animals, shooting animals, looking after animals, pet animals, animals to eat, animals to tend, animals to love.'

Old Mrs. Keal had been asked what she said when she came round from the anaesthetic after her amputation. 'Oh, I was very quiet. Very quiet, they said.' She

had thought herself back during the Great War when her husband was away at the Front 'and I was looking after 15 bullocks, and all I could think of was worrying whether they'd been fed all right. They say the last thing you think of before you go off is the thing you talk about, don't they? Though I don't remember thinking that.'

Ruefully, almost, Turner records that 'there is no inn in Luccombe, nor anywhere on the Acland Estate. The nearest is Wootton Courtenay. There is virtually no social centre in Luccombe beyond the doorstep and the village street. The parish hall, which was presented to the village after the First World War and is an old army hut, is rarely used now.'

He pictures a visit to Wootton Courtenay on a Saturday night to find three or four Luccombe men in the 'Dunkery' and names Bob Prescott, 'looking tired and weather-beaten, slumped up in a chair next to the bar; Mr. Hales who has cycled from Luccombe, sitting in a chair by the window; a man of 45 from Luccombe in the next-door chair; Mr. Keal, who has walked in, standing leaning on his cane.'

Talk is about horses but then progresses to how stony a field can be. 'Ay, that's the stoniest one you got, George, bain't it ...? Big stones ... One along of Dunkery be stonier ... Proper hard ... Never seed such big stone ... Stoniest I got.'

When they moved on to the chocolate ration, none predicted that it was going to last into the next decade – being finally abolished at Churchill's insistence shortly before the coronation of Queen Elizabeth II in 1953.

Sadly, their names are in the churchyard. It is Wootton Courtenay that has the best in the way of epitaphs, with the following rhyme to Mary Siderfin, who died in 1717:

'Here you may see where I do ly,
As you be now so once was I.
As I am now so shall you be,
Prepare therefore to follow me.'

THE WALK ≻≻≻

PARK AND start from the roadside car park beside the telephone kiosk to the north-east of Luccombe parish church, opposite Shamolee (Ordnance Survey map references SS 912 446).

Set off northwards, following the stream beside the eastern road out of the village.

Turn right at the bridge, towards Minehead, and follow the tarred lane for a mile to the junction of Blackford.

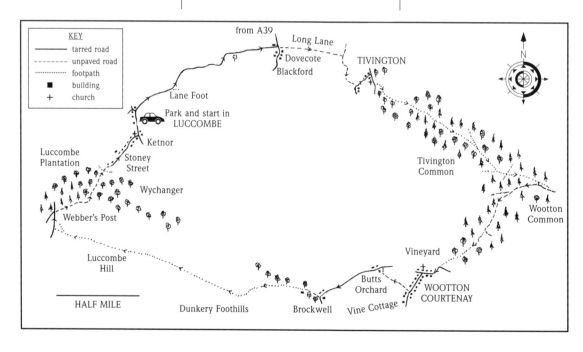

Opposite – Norman dovecote: under a corbelled roof, at Blackford

Right – Wooded slopes: overlooking Wootton Courtenay, with the Brendon Hills beyond

Below – Lone pine: framing a glimpse of Luccombe church, with the heights of Selworthy forming the skyline

Here we have a diversion, by turning right for 30 yards and then left, to visit the mediaeval dovecote at Blackford which is opened to the public by the National Trust. The 302 nest-hole Norman dovecote of 'Culver Close' – from the Saxon for dove, though it is currently doveless – in 'Blackford alias Tyvynton' is almost totally rock-built with a corbelled roof dome. It is attributed to 'fierce and licentious' Hugh of Avranches, created Earl of Chester by William the Conqueror, his putative uncle, who was nicknamed 'Hugh Lupus' from the wolf's head on his shield.

From the crossroads, as seen on our initial approach, we proceed straight ahead, into a double-hedged green lane which is signed for Tivington. Long Lane heads east, towards the woods of Tivington Heights.

In 600 yards we come to a junction of tracks at Long Lane Cross.

Turn right, to Tivington. Here we ford the stream and then turn left, uphill along a tarred road to the cob-walled thatched barn opposite Troytes Farm House. Note the pigeon holes in its next-door cottage wall.

Proceed to the junction, which is Tivington Cross. Here we turn right, uphill, to the 14th century St Leonard's Chapel-of-ease. It was restored in 1896 and has a post-Reformation cottage attached beside the road. The only thatched church in the diocese of Bath and Wells, it is doubly unusual in having an open fireplace. The bell over the door comes from the Acland family yacht, *The Lady of St Kilda*.

Ten yards up from the chapel cottage, called Dunkery View, we turn left, into a bridleway, uphill beside the wood. We are now heading south-east. Ahead we enter Tivington Plantation, and look back down the valley across Acland Country to the Bristol Channel at Porlock and white-painted Selworthy Church in the woods on the opposite hillside.

Continue proceeding ahead on entering the wood, and also keep straight on at woodland junctions. Next is Tivington Common, also tree-covered but still with some heather and bilberries beneath.

Here we leave National Trust land and enter a slightly more open mix of moorland and trees.

Turn left at a junction of tracks, south-eastwards, with trees to the left and a glimpse of a view to the right.

In 100 yards we continue straight ahead, towards Dunster. Also keep going straight ahead at the next two path junctions; with birch scrub to the left and beech trees to the right.

At the summit we pass an Ordnance Survey triangulation pillar, somewhat obscured by beech trees, on the bank to your right. Leftward is a view of Wales and the upper Bristol Channel, to Hinkley Point. This is gorse-smothered Wootton Common.

In 40 yards we turn right, to overlook a great panorama across the Brendon Hills, and then turn immediately right again in another ten yards.

We are now heading south-west, up and over the brow of the ridge and then down to Wootton Courtenay.

Fork left at the junction in 250 yards. Also fork left into the lesser option in a further 150 yards.

Timberscombe is the village down to the left, and Dunkery Beacon (back in Acland Country) tops the right-hand skyline, being at 1,704 feet the highest point in Somerset.

In 250 yards we fork right to cross a forest road and then fork left on the other side of it, into what is the third option from the right.

A footpath goes down through the trees, to Wootton Courtenay. Turn left in 75 yards, to zig-zag

through wilder woods. Continue straight ahead at a woodland crossroads.

On leaving the trees, at a stile, we descend across a field towards the centre of the village, with the vineyard of Pritchard's Winery on the south-facing slope to our right. Exit across the stile beside the gate and continue straight ahead, down the road.

We proceed uphill beside Rose Cottage to Manor Farm and All Saints parish church, with a churchyard cross, saddle-topped tower, and fine collection of roof bosses in the north aisle. The yew tree is estimated to be 700-years-old.

Turn left at the junction between the church and Old Rectory, downhill for 200 yards.

Turn right immediately after the junction, into a bridleway beside Vine Cottage, which implies continuity of grape growing here since the previous warmer climate of the Middle Ages.

The ferny deep-cut track has an active badger sett. Pass Butts Orchard and turn left along the tarred road, which climbs to Brockwell in half a mile.

Here we re-enter National Trust land, for the remainder of the walk, and bear right at the bend, westwards towards Luccombe and Dunkery.

Fork left beside the house and garden in 150 yards. We are now heading west, following the banked hedge on to the open moor, which is Luccombe Hill.

In theory we are heading west, but at present the only usable track bends further to the south, skirting the foothills of Dunkery Beacon.

Turn right at the junction of tracks, north-westwards, towards Webber's Post and Porlock Hill. The Holnicote Estate and our route so far spreads out to the right. It is a stony path for the next mile or more.

Webber's Post is a car park amid the pines. Keep going straight ahead along the main path and turn right on reaching the road.

In 150 yards, before reaching the road junction, we turn right beside the initial pine clumps.

A track is signed downhill to Luccombe, with conifers to your left and scrubby moorland to the right. We are heading north-east, via a gully with a stream, to Luccombe in a mile.

The village starts with The Cottage and the track becomes Stoney Street, bringing us to the Post Office ('Ketnor') and St Mary's parish church.

Your car is down to the left after the junction. ◆

Top – Roof lines: thatch, tiles and the church tower, at Luccombe

Left – Red berries: Luccombe's cotoneaster crop awaits the first fieldfares

Selworthy and Acland Country

JUSTIFYING ITS claim to be the most beautiful village in England, with a church and setting to match the hyperbole, Selworthy overlooks the great valley inland of Porlock. Facing south, this delightful place is protected from the coastal gales by the high shoulder of Selworthy Beacon. There are trees everywhere across these slopes and hollows.

Sounds abound as well as sights. Croaking at each other are the big black birds of the sky, the ravens, and the brown fowls of the air are buzzards. These are silent as they circle, perpetually it almost seems, but they mew like cats when they are with young. Woodpeckers drummed away in the woods when a pheasant caused me to jump at 17.45 hours that afternoon, a split second before a thud and a rumble.

A gentleman approaching with his dog must have realised that I was startled. 'That's Concorde, coming in from New York,' he reassured me. 'On a clearer day you'd be able to see her. You can tell the time by them.'

He also told me about the repercussions of the 1944 take-over of Selworthy by the National Trust; 'We exchanged one feudal landlord for another – how on earth could anyone be so enthralled by London life to decide to give all this away? Everything, for as far as you can see, and a lot more that you can't!'

The 37-year-old benefactor, fifteenth baronet Sir Richard Acland, was a Fabian socialist, who would be the post-war Labour MP for Gravesend and lived until 1991. He believed it was morally wrong for an individual to own or inherit all this wealth and beauty. In the words of the National Trust notice-board (which does not name him) he 'gave the village and all the land

visible to the south' – thousands of acres of valley fields and upland moors – to the nation.

That included his family seat, Holnicote House, which is the mansion that replaced 'the noble old manor of Sir Thomas Acland', destroyed by fire in 1779. Sir Richard walked away from it all, to live at Broadclyst, near Exeter.

The other Acland of special note was Sir Thomas, the tenth baronet, who created Selworthy as we admire it today. Despite a huge church and an exceptionally crowded churchyard, there were few houses in the village in 1828, when Sir Thomas decided to rebuild it as a model hamlet. He was so intrigued by something similar at Blaise Hamlet, Henbury, near Bristol, that he designed it 'as a refuge for estate pensioners'.

Building the collection of matching chocolate-box cottages

Round chimneys: cottage beside Selworthy churchyard

Leafy combe: sheltering Selworthy and its war memorial

provided a workface project for those hard times. They were made available to the staff and retainers on their retirement. As they are to this day, for the Trust still looks after its own, though no longer rent-free.

The Acland family also enhanced the estate with a series of viewpoint resting places, a few of which you visit in the course of this **four mile** walk.

All Saints parish church is also explored. Here again the Acland name is writ large. Apart from the memorials, look up to the comfortable south-facing upper storey over the porch – this was their balcony pew.

Architecturally impressive is the 45-feet-high embattled tower of about 1400. It is painted, like the cottages, but with what appears to be a purer white than the ubiquitous National Trust cream; it was a day of changing light and I had forgotten my Sandtex colour card. Set in the tower is an hour-striking clock, its mechanism a couple of centuries more recent than the walls.

Rarest of the treasures within is an ancient stone bowl, outwardly octagonal and a foot across, which was found in a hedge-bank at Howe's Close, half a mile to the east. Said to have been from the site of a Saxon or Viking burial mound, it is carved with two primitive Celtic faces, on opposite sides and alternating with a couple of simple crosses. This may well be one of the oldest fonts in the country.

Outside the church retains its mediaeval churchyard cross, somewhat weathered but otherwise in remarkably fine condition. Surrounded by dozens of clean-carved gravestones – give Selworthy a miss on resurrection day – it is 12 feet high and comprises an hexagonal three-stepped plinth, decorated square base, and chamfered shaft.

'I thought the students had gone back to Bristol,' a lady said from behind one of the stones, as I paced around the cross, counting its sides out loud after having miscounted the six into seven.

A student again! What a nice way of observing that I have entered my second childhood.

THE WALK ➤➤➤

TURN NORTH from the A39 Minehead to Porlock road at the 'Selworthy only' sign near Holnicote House, half a mile east of Allerford. You come to thatched cottages, a steep hill, and the church in half a mile. Continue up the lane for a further 100 yards and then turn left, into the 'National Trust Car Park' (Ordnance Survey map reference SS 922 468).

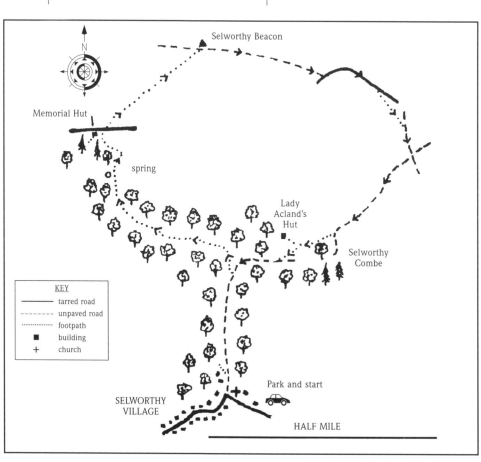

KEY
— tarred road
--- unpaved road
⋯ footpath
■ building
+ church

Selworthy Beacon

Memorial Hut

spring

Lady Acland's Hut

Selworthy Combe

Park and start

SELWORTHY VILLAGE

HALF MILE

Second summit: Selworthy Beacon, at 1,012 feet, is the twin peak of the Holnicote Estate

Walk back down to the church, or visit it on your return. Next you descend to the war memorial cross at the corner, above Selworthy Green, and turn right. The track is signed to 'Selworthy Beacon, Bury Castle, North Hill'.

Go through the gate and follow the main path, and stream, straight ahead up the wooded combe. In 400 yards you fork left, across the stream, on to a lesser track signed 'Selworthy Beacon ³/₄, Bury Castle 1'. To your left you pass the stone-walled boundaries of a mediaeval settlement.

In half a mile the rocky path rises from the tree-line of birch and pine, above a walled spring. Now there is gorse moorland to your right.

Then, in 120 yards to your left under the last of the pines, spot

Memorial Hut: in fact it is built like a mausoleum, beneath the last trees beside the open moor

the Memorial Hut. It is more of a red sandstone mausoleum than a hut, with inscriptions to Sir Thomas Dyke Acland (1787-1871):

'This spot was selected by his youngest surviving Son, JOHN BARTON ARUNDEL ACLAND of HOLNICOTE IN NEW ZEALAND, September 1878.'

Facing homeward is the explanation: *'IN REMEMBRANCE OF THE FATHER who, during more than fifty years, took Sunday walks up this combe with his CHILDREN AND GRANDCHILDREN training them in the love of NATURE and of CHRISTIAN POETRY this Wind and Weather Hut was built.'*

Each of the four sides is recessed with stone seats and further inscriptions, being verse from Keble on the 'deepening glen' and Hever on the 'beauty seen' to 'gild the span of ruin'd earth and sinful man'.

From here you continue across the road, along the dirt track opposite the 'Selworthy' pointer. In 500 yards, on the skyline at 1,012 feet above sea level, you arrive at the cairn which is Selworthy Beacon. It gives a classic view of the Bristol Channel, along the Devon and Somerset coast from Foreland Point to Steep Holm island, with the entire South Wales seaboard spread out ahead of you. Inland, the view peaks at Dunkery Beacon – the National Trust's ex-Acland sister hill.

Turn up-Channel along the stony track. You are heading towards Steep Holm and what little you can glimpse of Minehead, with the sea to your left. The path descends to the road, in 500 yards.

Turn left here, towards 'Selworthy, Dunster'. In 200 yards, on the other side of the bend, you turn right, again to 'Selworthy, Dunster'. Then in another 200 yards you turn right, once more towards 'Selworthy, Dunster'.

Follow this down the slope for 110 yards. Here, at the crossroads of rough tracks, you turn right – down the slope and now to 'Selworthy'. In a third of a mile the main track bends into the woods of Selworthy Combe.

Instead you continue straight ahead, along the narrower path, and walk up to Lady Acland's Hut. This summer house, in a fairy tale setting, was erected in about 1879 for Lady Gertrude Acland, wife of twelfth baronet Sir Charles. It was

restored in 1954 by the National Trust and is 'open to all for rest and shelter during daylight hours'. It is a timber chalet with an attractive circular chimney, in stone, but the fireplace has been bricked up.

Walk down the slope to the three former ponds, behind a series of stout dams, which are now semi-drained and covered with trees. Turn right to follow the track and the stream, beneath the big redwood and down a little bridge.

Here you rejoin the main track and turn right, down it. Hereon you keep the stream to your right and follow it to Selworthy.

After the gate, climb the flight of steps to the stone stile beneath the churchyard yew – for the perfect view of this picture postcard village. Then walk back through the churchyard to the far gate and return to your car. ◆

Above – High paths: the junction above Selworthy Combe

Below – Castle-like: the tower of Selworthy parish church

Bye Common and Great Staddon

Old wall: sprouting beech trees, at Nethercote

THE HEART of Exmoor, beside one of the remotest upstream sections of its main river, is explored on this **five mile** walk. It is buzzard and red deer country, far from the villages and with only isolated farmsteads and barns as its human intrusions.

These blend in quaintly, with minimal modernisms, and the overall feel is a walk through Somerset's big country. The scenery here is mainly fields and woods with remnants of ancient common land. There is a particularly precious wilderness beside the River Exe at Lyncombe Hill,

descending into a lush summertime landscape that contrasts totally with the heather heights.

The walk is along clear and well-marked paths, midway between Winsford and Exford, and is reached from the east – via the A396, which is the main north-south road from Dunster to Exbridge.

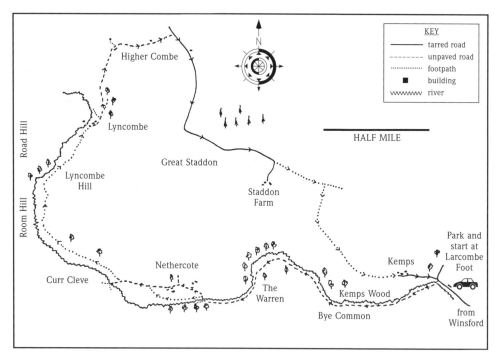

HALF MILE

First you find Wheddon Cross, and follow the words from there.

THE WALK ➤➤➤

TURN OFF the A396, westwards to Winsford, which lies three miles south of Wheddon Cross. Leave Winsford by the road signed to 'Exford'. This follows the River Exe.

A mile after the village you come to Larcombe Foot and Kemps Farm, with a layby at the corner of the left-hand side of the road (Ordnance Survey map reference SS 895 362).

Park and start from here, taking the left-hand of the two bridges, which is the one closest to Winscombe. This path crosses the main river and is signed 'Exford via Nethercote $4^1/_2$'. The track runs at the foot of the former Bye Common which has the dubious distinction of having been one of the steepest slopes to have been cleared of scrub and rocks during the grant-aided agricultural revolution. Extensive areas of bracken survive and it is still rabbit country – a mediaeval warren lay beside a curve of the river – which provides for the buzzards nesting on the other side of the water in the old oaks of Kemps Wood.

In a mile you turn right and cross the river, over a concrete bridge. Ignore the 'Exford' sign.

Then turn left on the other side, through a gate in twelve yards. This permissive path is also signed to 'Exford' and passes to the left of the

River Exe: which gives its name to the moor, passing Lyncombe

Humped bridge: west of Lyncombe but now leading nowhere

remote hamlet of Nethercote. Alternatively, you can stay on the main track, which is the right of way, and continue straight ahead through the twin farmyards of East and West Nethercote.

After passing West Nethercote the first path, beside the river, has a pointer, angled up the slope, which directs you into the top end of the following field. Here you turn sharply right, uphill, and re-join the main track.

The view to your left is dramatic, across the River Exe to Curr Cleeve and Room Hill.

Fork right, on to the upper option, as the stony track descends to a ford. The next mile, to Lyncombe, is through one of the remotest and most beautiful parts of Exmoor.

At Lyncombe you return to the world of neat green fields and drop down to the farm. Admire, but do not cross, the humped bridge.

After the farmyard you keep on the main track and then fork left, still keeping to the farm road, to follow the option which has blobs of blue paint as its marker. In half a

mile this brings you to a Victorian house at North Higher Combe.

Follow the 'Winsford via Staddon Hill' sign, which is the main track, to curve beside the house and then climb the hill. After a pair of barns you come to a junction on the hilltop.

Here you turn right, up Staddon-hill Road. This skirts the 1,265-feet summit of Great Staddon. To the left, behind your shoulder, is the greater peak of Dunkery Beacon.

Continue straight ahead at the point where the farm road turns right and drops down to Staddon Hill Farm, which is in a mile. Here you carry on along the now untarred track.

In 500 yards you turn right, into another green lane which is called Kemps Lane and descends to Kemps Farm, in a further mile. From here you continue downhill.

On crossing the bridge at the bottom you are back at your car. ◆

Fast flowing: the River Exe, in the heart of Exmoor

Jack Russells: heading down the valley from Lyncombe

River Exe: bridged at Winsford

Caratacus Stone and Winsford

RED DEER are quite likely to be on the menu for this **five mile** walk through Exmoor's hill country, up and down from 1,400 feet and across a magnificent tract of National Trust moorland. Buzzards will certainly be seen. There is also a civilised burst of mid-walk facilities in the quaint and cosy village-sized former town of Winsford.

It gives its name to the immense chunk of upland to the south, which is now doubly protected as common land registration number 175 and by National Trust ownership, which brings a freedom to roam.

Its historic centrepiece, shielded by a 1906-built 'bus shelter' canopy, is an inscribed stone from the Dark Ages. It is now called Caratacus Stone but appears in mediaeval documents, from 1219 onwards, as the Longstone.

This four feet high greyish-green monolith was used as a boundary marker for the Royal Forest of Exmoor – which was the king's hunting ground rather than a forest in the sense of being covered by trees.

It was not until 1890 that the boundary stone was discovered to be faintly inscribed, with debased Latin capital letters along the north-facing top side. These are each three inches across and read "CARAACI NEPUS' with the 'N' reversed. It means grandson, nephew or descendant of Caratacus or Caranacus, implying proud lineage from the last great Celtic chieftain, the King of the Silures, who was defeated by the Romans in the Welsh Marches in AD46.

The stone was uprooted and left lying on the ground by treasure hunters, testing out an ancient legend with no apparent reward, in October 1936. Subsequently, in 1937, an excavation showed that it does not mark a grave, and failed to find anything else of interest.

The Longstone was restored to its historic eastward tilt and set in concrete to discourage further exploration. Its lettering is similar in style to inscriptions of 5th or 6th century sub-Roman Christian Wales.

Not only is it an excellent starting point for the walk but landowner Sir Thomas Acland did us a favour in giving it such a distinctive canopy – for the spot would otherwise be almost unfindable. He also did the right thing and leased the whole common to the National Trust, for 500 years, in 1918.

That is just about in perpetuity, particularly as grandson Sir Richard Acland would give the rest of the Holnicote Estate to the Trust, in 1944.

THE WALK ⋙

WINSFORD HILL is a great expanse of upland, comprising 1,288 acres of open moorland in an irregular triangle

Caratacus Stone: now looking as if it is waiting for a bus

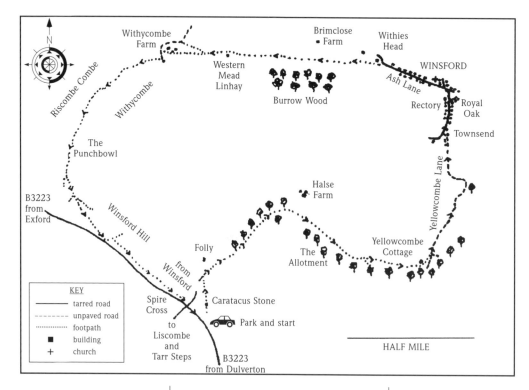

between Exford (7 miles northwest), Dulverton (5 miles southeast) and Winsford (1³/₄ miles north-east). Park and start from the middle of it, next to the B3223, from a layby just south of Caratacus Stone – beside the 'Bridleway Halse Lane' sign, which is 250 yards on the Dulverton side of Spire Cross (Ordnance Survey map reference SS 889 334).

Then head northwards, following a rushy ditch that leads to what looks like a bus-shelter, protecting Caratacus Stone. Continue to follow the ditch and then a track beside the fenced bank that is on the boundary of the common. The track and bank converge at a stony road and a gate, before you reach Folly House.

Big country: vapour trails mark the spot, amid heather and gorse on Winsford Hill

Turn right, through the gate, and walk straight ahead, following the path along the side of the hill. Head towards the silver communications tower on the distant skyline of the Brendon Hills.

At forks in the track we take the lower option, beside the valley trees. The public path follows the boundary of this bracken-smothered 'Allotment'. Follow it around the corner of the hill above Halse Farm. It becomes a well marked path, following the stream, and in half a mile brings us to a chalet.

Cross the water here and follow the fence beside Treetops and Yellowcombe Cottage. After the garden you turn left, uphill, and away from the stream.

This narrow track is Yellowcombe Lane, which goes up and over the hill, to Winsford village which is in half a mile. For some distance you are literally walking on bedrock as the double-hedge lane drops down to Townsend.

Turn right, down the tarred road, and pass the no-smoking Karslake House Hotel. Then turn left just around the corner, beside the Rectory and opposite the Royal Oak Inn – which had its smoking problem and burnt down in the winter of 1994 – to cross the cobbled packhorse bridge.

Turn left above Dowry Cottage and climb Ash Lane. St Mary's

61

Hill view: the village of Winsford has a town-sized history

parish church is to your right. There is a path into the churchyard a little way beyond the tower and tree. Inside is a sizeable and impressive coat of arms for James I, dated 1609, commanding 'curse not the King'.

Continue up the hill for 300 yards and then turn left, just before the corner and Withies Head. You follow the 'Footpath to Winsford Hill via Punchbowl 2'. On approaching the gates in twenty yards instead turn right – across the stile – and walk beside the grass, between the hedge-bank and the garden of Withies Head.

Hereon, after the next pair of stiles, the path continues straight ahead and heads into the upper valley. Cross the field to the right-hand of the two gates that face you on the other side.

Now follow the hedges straight ahead, keeping them to your left. Pass to the right of the ruin of Western Mead Linhay.

A mile from Winsford you pass through Withycombe Farm (or take the alternative route to the right of it).

On reaching the farm road you turn left and cross the stream. Then turn right, upwards, and follow the hedge along the spur of the hill, towards the wild land beyond.

In half a mile, at a point about 250 yards before the common, the bridleway goes through a gate and then turns left – so that the ancient hedge is now to your left for the final stage of the ascent across the sheep pastures. The Punchbowl, at the head of Withycombe, is to your left.

Walk straight ahead on re-entering National Trust moorland. This, once more, is Winsford Hill. Above the Punchbowl, at a crossroads of tracks, you turn left and then right, to follow one of the lesser options across this featureless heather and whortleberry wilderness.

If you come out on the road then turn left along it, downhill. Follow it back to your car – which is in half a mile. Take care not to drift northwards on to Halse Lane, or you will find yourself walking back to Winsford! Your car is beside the B3223. ◆

Tarr Steps and the River Barle

EXMOOR'S TARR STEPS are the biggest and best example of Britain's most primitive type of bridge. With 17 spans and a length of 180 feet it is a sophisticated form of stepping stones. The steps have evolved into stone piers bridged by great megalithic capstones weighing up to two tonnes apiece.

No cement is used and just sheer size, particularly the weight of the gritstone capping stones, holds the drystone structure together. Calling it 'drystone' is certainly a misnomer when the River Barle is swollen by melt-water, winter rains, or summertime flash-floods. In more normal times the footway along the top of Tarr Steps is three feet above the water. Clapper bridges are of unknown date and origin. They occur on Dartmoor, in the Cotswolds, and on both sides of the Pennines. It is tempting to regard them as prehistoric but some archaeologists say the more likely answer is that they date from the wool roads of the Middle Ages.

Tarr, however, has intrinsic antiquity as it is believed to derive from the Celtic word *tochar* for a causeway – which is the best description of the present structure over the Barle – so there was arguably something here in deeper history being, or looking much the same, to give the name. Furthermore the fording point for stock, immediately upstream of Tarr Steps, has been in use for thousands of years. It is still a public road and the Steps, which are legally regarded as the footway to it, are a county bridge maintainable by Somerset highways department.

Anyway, even if they might not be as old as they look, clapper bridges are well inside the requisite age bracket to qualify as ancient monuments. They also deserve preservation for being superbly picturesque. And they are environmentally vulnerable.

Despite its immensity, and those capstones are huge, all but one span of the original Tarr Steps were swept away in the disastrous Exmoor floods of August 1952 which devastated Lynton and Lynmouth. Fortunately, being so large, the stones did not get washed far and they were recovered for the restoration.

Each was numbered, just in case the bridge needed to be rebuilt again, and cables were slung upstream to try and hold back trees and branches and other flood debris. This had caught beneath the capstones and was then levered upwards and sideways by the force of the water to do most of the damage.

The bridge must have been deserted by its guardian angel. He is said to be the devil, who erected Tarr Steps so that he could sunbath and paddle his feet in the water. Having vowed to destroy any creature that tried to cross, he took a cat as his sacrifice, but was then

Washed away: Tarr Steps were reconstructed after the flash-flood of 1952

confronted by a parson who gave as good as he got when it came to mouthing profanities. The devil relented over sole usage but retained bathing rights.

These days the sunshine is dappled as some of the densest woods in the county have closed in along the gorge-like sides of the River Barle. Mostly sessile oak, they were formerly coppiced for bark, stripped and used in tannin-making for the leather industry, and to provide charcoal. This cropping tends to give the trees a wide rootstock. Scrub birch, ash, hazel, and wych elm proliferates on the rocky slopes. Mammals range in size from dormice, in the hazel, to red deer. Breeding birds include redstart, wood warbler and pied fly-catcher, through to buzzard and raven. Watch out for dippers, grey wagtails, and the occasional kingfisher working the waterline.

Eighty-five species of flowering plants have been recorded between Withypool and Dulverton but the more notable speciality vegetation is in the form of the lush bryophytes and lichens that coat

Uncertain future: Well Farm represents hill farming in jeopardy, as it crumbles beneath the moss

and drape the branches of the trees. Tree lungwort is the supreme parasite of the older oaks.

Violets in the semi-clearings of bracken provide food for caterpillars of three species of fritillary butterflies. Just about everywhere wild on this **five mile** walk is a site of special

scientific interest designated by English Nature.

THE WALK ⋙

LISCOMBE AND Tarr Steps are signposted south from the B3223, four miles northwest of Dulverton. The car park for Tarr Steps, provided by the Exmoor National Park authority, is a short distance down the hill after the hamlet of Liscombe (Ordnance Survey map reference SS 873 324).

Just inside the roadside hedge, at the lower end of the car park, is the 'Scenic Footpath to Tarr Steps'. It descends to cross the Little River and then follows a terrace above the stream. You look across to Tarr Farm.

In 500 yards the path drops down to re-cross the stream, with a choice of bridge or stepping stones, and then you cross the wide River

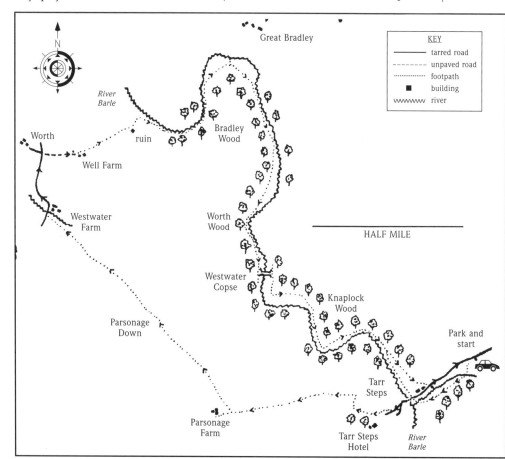

Stepping stones: of megalithic proportions, not that it stopped all but one being washed away in the Lynmouth disaster

Barle, over the ancient and ramshackle Tarr Steps.

Once across you continue ahead for just 20 yards and then turn right, up the drive to 'Tarr Steps Hotel'. This is also the path to 'Withypool Hill 2$\frac{1}{2}$' which forks to the right of the laurel bushes beside the hotel gate. The track goes uphill steeply, brings you through a gate, into a sloping pasture.

Make sure you turn left inside the second corner of this field. Keep the power line to your left and the hedge to your right.

Continue straight ahead from the third corner of this field and also carry straight on from the gate in the corner of the next field.

Turn right beside the penultimate gate before Parsonage Farm without going through it. This point is just over half a mile from Tarr Steps.

Having turned right we stay inside the same field and continue to keep a banked hedge to our left. We are now heading north-west, continuing towards Withypool Hill.

Keep going straight ahead as you come to gates or stiles. In a mile we reach a tarred road, beside the stream at Westwater Farm.

Turn right, across the bridge, and follow Worth Lane uphill, around a double bend, for a quarter of a mile.

You come to an unsigned crossroads that is at Worth. Turn right here, away from the farm, and take the unpaved option between beech hedges and next to an electricity pole.

Fork left at Well Farm barns, following the left-hand hedgerow downhill to a hunting gate and then into a wooded valley. Towards the bottom you pass a mossy ruin that was the old Well Farm. The spring still rises beside it. The bridleway goes through a hunting gate and fords it diagonally, straight ahead, to a five-barred gate on the other side. It can be fast flowing and deep.

Instead, I went through the gate but then followed the right-hand riverbank downstream. Others do the same, as is evident from the well-walked path beside Bradley Wood.

From here, beneath the spectacularly sited Great Bradley, we are again following rights of way as well as the river. The path is across the pasture 100 yards from the sound of the Barle.

You then converge with the river and follow a picturesque rocky terrace. In half a mile, having virtually walked in the water beneath Worth Wood, you cross a footbridge to the east bank.

Turn right on the other side. Cross the open grassland and then a stream immediately after a gate. The path is now signed, straight ahead: 'Tarr Steps $^1/_2$'.

After the waterside rock path and the bend in the river, around Knaplock Wood, the main path rises on to a terrace. From here you can either follow the yellow markers to Tarr Bridge, or fork left on to the 'Bridleway'. The latter joins the tarred road at a metal gate beside Tarr Farm.

Either way you turn left and walk back to the car park. ◆

Above – Valley setting: Tarr Steps Farm in one of the few breaks in the sessile oakwoods

Below – Two rivers: Tarr Farm looks down the double valleys of the Little River and the River Barle

Anstey Commons and Hawkridge

Bridleway marker: with Exmoor to the left and Dartmoor to the right, on the Two Moors Way

THE DEVON parishes of East Anstey, West Anstey, and Molland have immense areas of common land, preserved as open moorland, which merge into a continuous tract of wilderness several miles wide. They form the southern edge of Exmoor National Park to the west of Dulverton.

Southwards are deep-cut Combe Woods and Gourte Wood and a view stretching to Dartmoor. The moors are largely featureless but that adds to the significance of the occasional landmarks, such as the Froude Hancock Memorial Stone, the Bronze Age Long Stone, and contemporary West Anstey Barrows. There is also a slate to George Stapleton, a huntsman, whose red deer herd usually outnumbers the humans on these great commons.

Northwards, marking the Somerset boundary, is Dane's Brook and the isolated village of Hawkridge, standing at 950 feet, which is notable for Norman fittings in its church, including an aristocratic memorial stone discovered in the walls, and brought back to the village after having resided in South Molton and St Nicholas Priory, Exeter.

This **nine mile** walk enters more deep-cut wooded gullies at West Hollowcombe Wood and Venford Wood. Your first crossing of the Dane's Brook, approaching Zeal Farm, is across a ford – so expect wet feet.

THE WALK >>>

APPROACH THE Anstey Commons from the Exmoor National Park boundary at Five Cross Ways, two miles west of Dulverton, and head westwards along Ridge Road towards Molland. In a mile and a half we cross a cattle grid to enter Anstey Money Common, on the north side of the road, and Woodland Common, south of it.

Park and start in the informal parking area in the gorse bushes beside the bridleway sign 200 yards west of the cattle-grid, on the northern side of Ridge Road (SS 857 289).

Set off southwards, across the road, downhill across Woodland Common towards West Anstey and Dartmoor, which forms the distant skyline.

In 500 yards we approach a gate and cattle grid beside the road junction at Badlake Moor Cross.

Do not leave Woodland Common but instead, on reaching the trees, turn right along the unfenced road along its southern edge.

Follow the road to the aged pines of Woodland Plantation in a mile where the road bends to the left, across the cattle-grid, to enter the pastures of West Anstey.

In 300 yards we turn right, north-westwards, along a cul-de-sac lane to East Ringcombe in 400 yards.

Follow the farm track around to the right as it approaches the buildings. Turn left to pass the house, and west across the field to the west of it, for 250 yards.

At the end of the field beyond the house we go into the top corner and through the left-hand pair of gates.

We now follow the power cables and the left-hand hedge bank, around and above springs in a combe, to enter Ringcombe, in 400 yards. Here we go through the first part of the

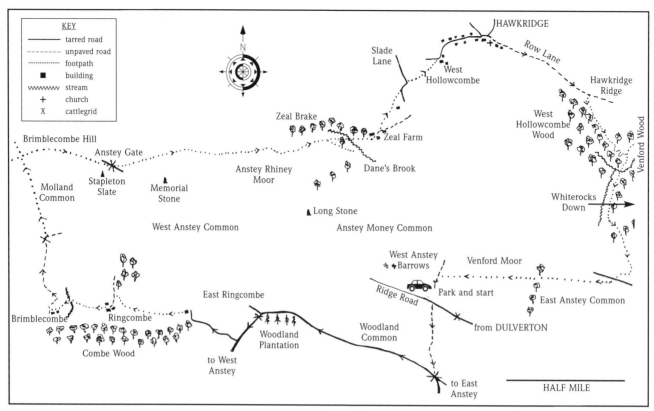

Map key:
KEY
— tarred road
--- unpaved road
···· footpath
■ building
wwww stream
+ church
X cattlegrid

Map labels: HAWKRIDGE, Slade Lane, Row Lane, West Hollowcombe, Hawkridge Ridge, West Hollowcombe Wood, Venford Wood, Zeal Brake, Zeal Farm, Brimblecombe Hill, Anstey Gate, Anstey Rhiney Moor, Dane's Brook, Whiterocks Down, Molland Common, Stapleton Slate, Memorial Stone, Long Stone, West Anstey Common, Anstey Money Common, West Anstey Barrows, Venford Moor, East Anstey Common, Ridge Road, Park and start, from DULVERTON, East Ringcombe, Brimblecombe, Ringcombe, Combe Wood, Woodland Plantation, to West Anstey, Woodland Common, to East Anstey, HALF MILE

farmyard and then up into the main yard.

Exit along the left-hand side of the lambing shed and follow the hedge-bank straight ahead, westwards, keeping it on your left for the next three fields.

In 250 yards we go through the gate across the stream and then

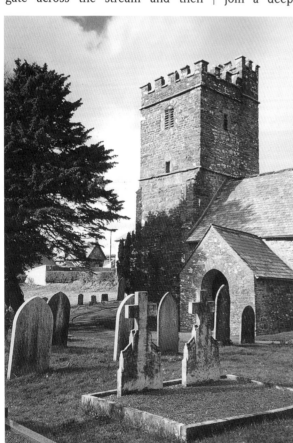

Left – Windy ridge: Hawkridge is aptly named, high on the southern extremity of Somerset

Right – Plentiful name: best-carved for some 20 stones to the Westcott family in Hawkridge churchyard

follow the power cables south-westwards, up the slope to Brimblecombe, overlooking the double valleys of Combe Wood and Gourte Wood.

Follow its right-hand fence. Immediately after the buildings, at a junction of paths, we turn right and join a deep-cut track that climbs northwards out of the combe. Follow it around the bends and across the pastures for 700 yards.

Here we enter the open moorland of the Molland Estate, with Anstey's Gully and Anstey's Combe down to our left. This is Molland Common, which becomes a great featureless plateau, stretching for

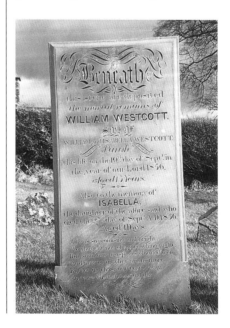

two miles to the Devon-Somerset county boundary at the two Willingford Bridges.

Continue straight ahead into the moor. In theory we are heading north-by-northwest (film buffs will visualise Alfred Hitchcock boarding a green bus). In 700 yards there is an intersection of bridleways before we reach the unfenced Ridge Road. Whether you find the spot, however, is another matter as walkable paths are at a premium in this wilderness and you have to go with what you find.

Either way we need to bear right (or turn right on reaching the road if you overshoot) to climb the gentle heather-covered slope for 800 yards to the cattle grid in the hedge-bank at Anstey Gate on Brimblecombe Hill. We are now heading eastwards. You may spot the memorial slate to 'George H. Stapleton, 1920-93, Gone away hunting.' Quite likely you will have seen stags by now.

Cross the cattle-grid and then bear left, along a peaty moorland track signed as the 'Bridleway to Hawkridge'. The conspicuous monolith on the ridge is a massive eight-feet high Memorial Stone to P. Froude Hancock in whose name a block of moorland was 'Subscribed to by over 500 of his friends'. This is West Anstey Common with Anstey Rhiney Moor forming its damper and lower northern slopes.

Proceed eastwards for a mile, descending into the wooded gully

Burial mound: one of the West Anstey Barrows, on an otherwise featureless tract of common land

Long Stone: Bronze Age megalith at the head of a combe above Zeal Farm

west of Zeal Farm. To the right, looking up a scrubby combe, the 4-feet high slimline Long Stone of Bronze Age vintage is silhouetted on the southern skyline.

The bridleway fords the Dane's Brook below and behind a patch of birch scrub to the west of the Zeal Farm. If there is too much water for stepping stones then wade across rather than jumping between the rocks. It is safer to get wet feet.

On the other side a stony track climbs into rustic Zeal Farm, passing through the yard between the house and a hillside pond.

On the other side we continue straight ahead into the next field and ignore the farm access track to our right. Go through the gate into the field above the outlying stone and slate barn.

Bear left across this field to the double bend in Slade Lane. We are heading north-east.

From the other side of the second bend we go through a gate and then proceed straight ahead, up and over the hill to the far corner of the field in 300 yards, to the left of West Hollowcombe.

Walk up the second of the double bends and continue north-eastwards, into the field, following the bank to the gate to the left of West Hollowcombe.

This is the western end of Hawkridge village and we proceed to the junction at the Pump Tree (a beech) and pass the shop window of Moor View (offering antlers for sale). Incidentally, as I was reminded by Colin Hodge from stalking country near Oban, antlers are rare finds in the wild because the stags chew them to re-cycle scarce trace elements. Next is St Giles's parish church. Its treasures are a huge rough-hewn Norman font, in local red sandstone, and a much more finely carved foliated limestone coffin lid. Discovered in the wall behind the pulpit, this was re-set to guard the parish safe. Bevelled edges are inscribed in Norman French, apparently commemorating William de Plessy, Lord of the Manor and the King's Bailiwick of the Forest of Exmoor, who died in 1274. Architecturally, the notable churchyard memorial is the wordy 1856 slate to William Westcott 'of this Parish'. Some two dozen other Westcotts lie here; several listing placenames such as Draydon, Hill Farm, Shircombe, and Zeal, where we have walked. They are not unique, in that just a few family names account for most of the graves, in a setting that looks south from Somerset to the moors of Anstey Commons.

Leave the tarred road at the junction beside the churchyard gate to head south-east along Row Lane which is signed to Dulverton and East Anstey Common. The latter is our penultimate objective.

In 800 yards, at the end of the first field, we turn right on Hawkridge Ridge, into the gorse bushes in the corner.

Here a gate takes us into West Hollowcombe Wood. We descend along its northern boundary for 350 yards, as we head south-east, and then follow the track as it bends to the right, down into the scrubby trees. We zig-zag towards the sound of the babbling brook.

Turn right at the junction of woodland paths and re-cross Dane's Brook at the ford and footbridge, 150 yards to the south-west.

Beyond we climb southwards above the sessile tree-line of Venford Wood, keeping a tributary down to our right.

In 350 yards we enter the scrubby slopes of Whiterocks

Down. We continue heading south.

Go through the tree-height beech hedge into the higher pasture of Whiterocks Down where we bear right, south-eastwards, up to its corner in 250 yards

In the following field the bridleway bears right, south-westwards, to cross the rushy pasture.

Walk up to the gates in the beech hedges either side of the road beside East Anstey Common.

Having crossed into this common, which is designated access land, we bear right. We are now walking westwards.

On the far side we go through a hunting gate in the hedge-bank, the ancient boundary between the two Anstey parishes, 100 yards up from the far right-hand corner of East Anstey Common.

On the other side we continue westwards, uphill across Venford Moor. Keep its northern boundary to your right for 800 yards.

Go through the gate in the hedge and then turn left, southwards up and over the brow of the hill, to your car in 250 yards. Across to your right, 300 yards north-west, are the Bronze Age burial mounds of West Anstey Barrows, if you still have the energy for a final diversion. ◆

Top – Memorial Stone: erected in 1933 as a tribute to P. Froude Hancock

Left – Boundary marker: beside the moorland memorial to P. Froude Hancock, who had more than 500 paying friends

Town church: All Saints at Dulverton is sandwiched between a hillside and the woods

LORNA DOONE stands in bronze outside the police station in the west Somerset town of Dulverton which proclaims itself 'The Gateway to Exmoor'. Professor George Stephenson's life-size figure gives three-dimensional reality to the literary tradition created by London barrister Richard Doddridge Blackmore.

She was his third book, in 1865, and an instant best-seller – doing for Exmoor what Sir Walter Scott had achieved for the Highlands. The historical romance is set in the 17th-century and tells the story of Lady Lorna Dugal, kidnapped in childhood by the outlaw Doones of Badgworthy.

Its setting is genuine enough as are some of the tales, embellished by the lawyer's romantic imagination but having their origin in legends of feuds and banditry that had endured in the oral folk tradition of the hill country. Stories of highwayman Tom Faggus and his strawberry mare, Winnie, pre-date Blackmore's novel. There is a 'Faggus Mead' in woods near Monksilver and 'Faggus Stable' in Chargot Wood, Luxborough.

These days such snippets of folklore are regarded as suspect, seldom having retained an independent existence, being merged with the literary associations. 'It's all Lorna Doonery now!' Sir William Halliday, of Glenthorne, used to say.

The creator of it was none too happy at the resultant over-attention that was being bestowed on the landscape. Having shared the countryside of his schooldays with the great British public, which now found it accessible via the Devon and Somerset branch of the Great Western Railway, Blackmore retreated from it and the unwanted attentions of his admirers. He died in 1900, 'proud, shy, reticent, and by no means easy of access'. Travelogues were celebrating his Doone Country as 'The Blackmore Country' and societies were formed in his name.

Charabancs became coaches but a new visual focus was needed for the age that had turned away from the word. His heroine's statue in Dulverton would be commissioned by Dr. Whitman Pearson, an American, and given to the town in 1990.

The railway has gone, and indeed was held back by the hostile geography to a 'Dulverton' station that was in fact in the village of Brushford, two miles south-east. It is preserved in an attractive time-warp beside the Carnarvon Arms. Apart from the trains, the scene is as unchanged and as emphatically picturesque as it was in Blackmore's Day.

Quaint corners abound and are hemmed in by a backdrop of grandeur. Wooded slopes, virtually a precipice for the most part, rise 600 feet from the River Barle which tumbles over a rocky floor. It is a landscape of special 'trophy' wildlife as is evidenced by stuffed specimens in the human watering holes. Trout and salmon are at the bottom. Red deer come next. Buzzards mew above; sometimes assuming the size of eagles when surprised on the ground.

This **four mile** walk is a circuit of the gorge north of the town, and inevitably involves one stiff climb, but is otherwise easy going as all the tracks are firm and clearly defined.

THE WALK ⪼⪼⪼

PARK IN the town, which is at the riverside junction of the B3223 with the B3222 (Ordnance Survey map reference SS 913 278).

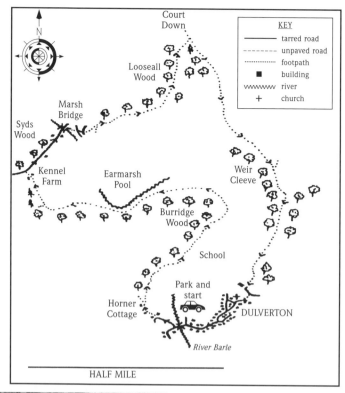

Start from the Bridge Inn, in the main street, and cross the narrow humped bridge, of five pointed arches, over the River Barle. Turn right immediately on the other side, along a lane with a sign 'Paths to (No Cars) ...' and a number of destinations.

Fork right in 150 yards, uphill between the thatched Rose Cottage and slated Berry House. Then fork right again in 50 yards, keeping The Mount and High Corner to your left.

The road narrows and climbs a gully. In a further 50 yards, at Horner Cottage, it forks again and you continue straight ahead – along the track signed to 'Tarr Steps, Hawkridge'. We pass a memorial plaque to Miss B. K. Abbot and Auberon Herbert, recording that through their generosity a large part of Burridge Woods 'was purchased and later handed over to the Exmoor National Park for management in the interests of public enjoyment for all time'.

Fast flowing: ferns, foliage and rocks in an identikit picture of the Barle

Lorna Doonery: as the locals call it, spilling over from Doone Country proper to a statue guarded by Dulverton police

It is mainly oak, with holly, rhododendron and ferns beneath. In half a mile you walk beside the boulder-strewn river and then climb on to a path that winds along a terrace above it.

Next, after a brief return to the riverbank at Earmarsh Pool, the path turns inland and brings us to a junction of woodland tracks.

Fork right here, following the pointer to 'Tarr Steps'. The path emerges in a great clearing in the valley bowl and passes between the outbuildings of Kennel Farm.

Turn right at the tarred road, following it downhill to the wrought-iron Marsh Bridge.

Turn right on the other side, on to the track that goes over the delightful packhorse bridge beneath beech trees.

On the other side you return to the road at a junction. Continue straight ahead, uphill, to another junction on the slope in 25 yards.

Carry on across this road as well, onto a stony uphill track signed to 'Court Down'. In 75 yards it joins another trackway and you continue straight ahead, uphill.

In a third of a mile, after Looseall Wood, we are at the 1,000 feet contour and come to a junction of tracks on the lip of Court Down.

Turn right here, beneath the tall fir trees. This attractive double-hedged track then enters open countryside and gradually descends south-eastwards to the next wooded hillside which is in half a mile, at Weir Cleeve.

In another half mile, at an accelerating pace of descent, we are suddenly back in Dulverton, beside the gates of 'Dulverton V.C. First School'.

White-walled: picturesque pedestrian corner of old Dulverton

Forty yards after these gates you turn right, down steps and along an alleyway to the gravestone of surgeon Charles Palk Collyns (1793-1864): 'He resided for fifty years in this parish, relieving pain succouring the poor promoting local improvements upholding manly pursuits and actively performing the duties of a loyal Englishman.'

After visiting All Saints Church, 'the largest in Exmoor Country,' you may think differently of Collyns and the Victorian improvers. For what it offers in terms of size it lacks in interest, as all but the tower date from a total rebuilding of 1855.

You drop into the historic market town at Bank Square and Fore Street. This becomes the High Street and returns you to Bridge Inn. ◆

Feeding time: in the River Barle, in the shadow of Dulverton Bridge

Wimbleball and Lake Dam

Water wall: Wimbleball Dam took several years to build and was completed in 1979

SOMERSET'S BIGGEST dam is a monumental construction, worthy of the Elan Valley in central Wales, that must qualify as Exmoor's greatest man-made creation. It also has a level of public access that is a world away from old fashioned attitudes towards reservoirs – indeed a permissive path runs along the very top of the 160-feet high concrete wall with Wimbleball Lake stretching away on one side and a colossal aerosol of spray watering the trees in the gorge below.

Haddon Hill car park has been provided by the Exmoor Park Authority so that you can walk down to the lake shore and its stupendous dam. They lie at the southern foot of the Brendon Hills, between Watchet and Bampton.

Built between 1974 and 1979, with the official opening in 1980,

Wimbleball Dam holds back 4,750,000,000 gallons of water. Now in the ownership of South West Water plc, it is the primary reserve supply for Bridgwater, Taunton, Tiverton and Exeter, and kept them going during the dry summers of 1989-90. Water covers 375 acres; half a square mile.

Information boards make more of the fact that it also releases essential year-round flows into the River Haddeo that in turn join the River Exe and keep that trickling through Devon. 'Without this water the Exe would have gone dry this summer,' a father was telling his two sons in an impromptu lecture from the dam wall, 'so it is essential for your beloved otters'. He did not add that the main reason our rivers run dry is because of water abstraction in the first place.

Dame Sylvia Crow, a landscape architect, has been given the credit for the trees and other refinements to the setting, though the inspiration is all around and has been provided by nature. Lady Harriet Acland appreciated it two centuries ago and created Lady Harriet's Drive – down which our **five mile** walk progresses – from Bury and through the now flooded valley to distant parts of her huge estate.

The lake has captured a mile of the deep-cut valley of the River Haddeo, eastward to the B3190 at Upton, but the great expanse of water comes in two wider arms that stretch northwards for a couple of miles. The biggest inundation spreads across the gentler scenery to Withiel Florey, a hamlet with a whitewashed church, and the slopes of Blagdon

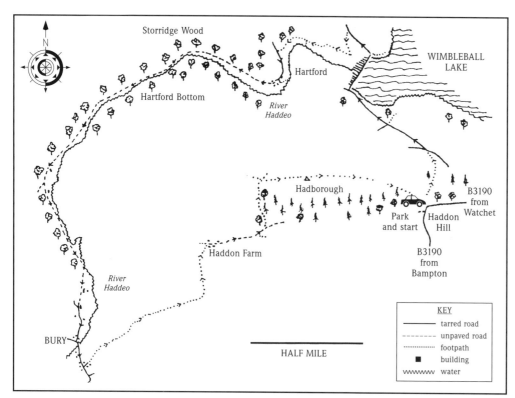

KEY
- ———— tarred road
- – – – – unpaved road
- ·········· footpath
- ▪ building
- wwwww water

HALF MILE

From above: the River Haddeo being released from Wimbleball Dam

Hill which is a south-facing spur of the Brendons.

Some 400 acres of Haddon Hill are owned by the National Park and public access has also been negotiated across the adjoining moorland.

This expanse conceals one of the authority's two herds of Exmoor ponies, the archetypal Celtic horse, which have hardly changed since the Ice Age. They were given rare breed status in 1981 and are shy and secretive, even in their sanctuary here. When you do glimpse them you may be surprised at how small there are – and how short their Iron Age riders must have been – as both mares and stallions are under 12.3 hands (124 centimetres).

I missed the other excitement – seeing it only momentarily between two herons above the Hartford trees – which was an RAF Hercules C130 transport aircraft, from Lyneham, which had skimmed the lake from the east in an imitation of Guy Gibson's dambusting 617 Squadron exploits. Being a four-engined turbo-prop, the Hercules is the closest thing in today's skies to the Lancasters of Bomber Command.

From below: propelled by 160-feet of water pressure, the River Haddeo spouts from concrete

If you want that sort of thrill, remember that the RAF never flies at weekends.

Finally, before you set off for Haddon Hill, a note about that intriguing name of Wimbleball. It apparently comes from 'windle' which is a crested dog's tail grass common hereabouts. 'Ball', meaning a rounded spur, perfectly describes the Upton Farm hillock that overlooks the lake from the other side.

THE WALK ➤➤➤

TURN NORTH off the B3190 at the sharp bend on Haddon Hill, which is between Ralegh's Cross and Bampton (Ordnance Survey map reference SS 970 285).

The Exmoor National Park Authority car park is screened behind the trees and has some severe traffic-calming ramps. It is partially deprived of its view of Wimbleball Lake by a bank of earth.

Go through the gate, on to the moor, and head northwards, towards the water. You pass beside a solitary outlying Scot's pine and then descend left of centre.

Fork right on joining the water company's access road and then continue downhill along it.

Fifty yards after the cattle-grid we turn right and cross the dam. To your left, both the main spout and the twelve-step spillway can perform sensationally.

The drop is said to be a few inches in excess of 160 feet and is sufficient to grip most people's stomachs.

Turn left on the other side, along the path signed towards Brompton Regis. In 250 yards we leave the concrete road and turn sharply left, down a stony track that drops between two ancient walls which support tree-sized beech hedges.

You are now heading towards Hartford hamlet and Bury village. As the track bends at the corner you have a full frontal view of the dam wall and may well sample its spray-zone, which can be a pleasure or pain depending upon the day's temperature.

After the next bend you continue straight ahead, through a field gate, and come to a second gate beside the River Haddeo. There is then a ford across a tributary, with a footbridge to its right.

Turn left along the tarred road on the other side, towards Bury.

First you pass through Hartford, which comprises Hartford Mill then Hartford Lodge. The latter is notable for summer flowers and an amazing garden wall, capped by quartz boulders.

After Hartford Trout Farm, Lady Harriet's Drive continues through Hartford Bottom. It is now a dirt track, with the River Haddeo on one side, the left, and Storridge Wood on the other.

It is a full two miles before it is tarred again, after lodge gates, for the final length down into Bury.

Turn left after the Old School House and Church House, over the cobbled packhorse bridge beside a wide ford. After the Forge and Haddeo View we come to Barn End and an 1889-dated chapel with an inscription from scripture.

Stop here, and don't continue any further towards the telephone

box and the road junction. Instead we turn left, immediately opposite Barn End, beside Chilcott's Bury which is the house with the round chimney.

Walk uphill, between Pixton Barn and Rockspray. Continue straight ahead, through the gate, up the deep-cut rocky track. It is double hedged and brings us to Haddon Farm in a mile.

Here you continue ahead, by going left and then immediately right, passing beside the back wall of the farmhouse. Keep the main building to your right.

About 300 yards after the farm, in Hadborough Plantation, turn left across a stile and enter the woods. Continue ahead, through the edge of the plantation, and keep going until you reach the open moorland on the brow of the hill, in 300 yards.

Here you turn right and pass Hadborough Ordnance Survey pillar. At 1,164 feet above sea level this is the high point of the walk. It also has a view, to the left, of the northern length of Wimbleball Lake, with the Brendon Hills beyond.

In half a mile, immediately after Hadborough Plantation, you turn right through a gate and are back in the car park. ◆

Bury Bridge: cobbled arches with a ford beside and church beyond

Modern lakeland: Exmoor's biggest expanse of inland water, seen from Haddon Hill, with the Brendon Hills in the distance

Clatworthy Reservoir and Castle

THERE IS a lakeland amid the southern folds of the Brendon Hills. It is the result of our demand for water and the fact that the Somerset uplands record an average of 50-inches of rain. Water and woods mix well in these hills, particularly around Clatworthy where a concrete dam was constructed by Holland Hannen and Cubitts (Great Britain) Limited for Taunton Borough Council between 1957-59.

This holds a lake of 130 acres with a maximum depth of 96 feet, and capacity of more than a billion gallons of water. The almost precise figure is 1,180,000,000 gallons.

The lake and its 24-inch main to Maundown Filter Station was opened by Princess Alexandra of Kent on 6th July 1961. It drains 4,500 acres around the head of the River Tone, which has its source at Beverton Pond in the Brendon Hills. These waters are stocked with brown and rainbow trout with the fly-fishing season being from April to mid-October.

Expanses of water also attract birds. My sightings were Canadian geese – grazing as a herd rather than a flock – mallard, raven, buzzard, jay, crow, swallow, wagtail plus the inevitable smaller things I am incapable of identifying. Squirrels don't quite qualify for the list but were also present in the trees.

Historically, the gem is Clatworthy Castle, which is a formidable Iron Age hill-fort of around the 3rd century BC. It has stout eastern defences but the other side, overlooking what was then the green valley of the River Tone, needed much less in the way of ramparts as the precipitous slope was 'scraped' instead, to present attackers with a vertical wall of rock.

Erosion and trees have lessened the visual effect but it remains a commanding location, enhanced if anything by being immediately above the dam and midway along the lake's higher slopes.

Unusually for these walks, we are going to be using permissive paths rather than rights of way. Therefore the by-laws and regulations of Wessex Water apply, rather than highway law; this meant that their vegetation did not feel the full vigour of my secateurs and pruning-saw.

Open hours are currently posted as 08.00 to sunset. Note 'No dogs allowed on this site'. For further information ring Wessex Water on 01-345-300-600.

The dam: holds back more than a billion gallons of water

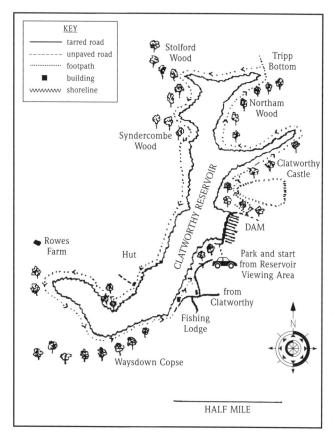

KEY
— tarred road
----- unpaved road
········· footpath
■ building
wwwww shoreline

Stolford Wood
Tripp Bottom
Northam Wood
Syndercombe Wood
Clatworthy Castle
CLATWORTHY RESERVOIR
DAM
Rowes Farm
Hut
Park and start from Reservoir Viewing Area
from Clatworthy
Fishing Lodge
Waysdown Copse

N

HALF MILE

Somerset area officers of the Ramblers' Association might like to check the status and route of two bridleways which are shown by the Ordnance Survey as running beside the northern and southern shorelines. I saw no signs of horse use and both paths have notices proclaiming 'This is a permissive path'.

Not that it affects our **four mile** walk because for the most part we have to use what are definitely only permissive paths. It is disappointing that the creators of this lake were allowed to drown public highways without providing a proper circuit of alternative paths around the edge. 'We can't do that – people pee in water!' That used to be the attitude but we live in more enlightened times – I think.

THE WALK ⪢⪢⪢

BEGIN FROM the Clatworthy Reservoir Viewing Area. This is hardly the easiest spot on earth to find, so it may be helpful to provide directions, from the A361 between Taunton and Bampton.

Turn north at the traffic lights in Wiveliscombe, into the town centre. Follow this road around to the left at the top of the hill and then turn right, beside the White Hart Hotel.

In a mile you drive up the village street at Langley Marsh (not that it possesses a sign, but the Three Horseshoes is conspicuous). Continue through the next village, in three miles, which is Huish Champflower and much better signed.

Follow the signs to 'Clatworthy Reservoir'. On reaching the edge of Clatworthy village you turn left to 'Reservoir Viewing Site'.

There are plenty of blue Wessex Water signs and ours is in 0.7 mile, at the top of the hill, where you turn right and enter 'Clatworthy Viewing Area and Nature Trail'. Drive to the end of its access road.

Park and start from the Viewing Area, beside the commemorative stone (Ordnance Survey map reference ST 043 310). Pay your parking fee and set off towards the water. Follow the path down to the dam and then walk across it. There is a series of fishponds in the valley below.

On the far side of the dam you turn right, for 75 yards, to the gate with multiple off-putting notices – 'No public right of way ... trespassing prohibited ... No public access'. Beside these you turn left, following a 'Nature Trail' arrow uphill into the trees. This is the scenic path through Clatworthy Wood, carpeted with bluebells, foxgloves and ferns, and along the top of the slope it passes beside the ditch and rampart of an Iron Age hill-fort. These defended the plateau above. Though unnamed on the map this fort is known locally as Clatworthy Castle.

As the bank bends to the right you continue straight ahead, for 50 yards, to a junction with the main woodland ride. Turn right along it. The lake is now occasionally visible to your left, as it will be for the rest of the walk. This woodland is more than two centuries old and used to be part of the Carew family's Clatworthy Estate.

After the gate we cross bracken-covered slopes and go around the red mud of a boggy backwater.

Southern shore: with fishing lodge and Waysdown Copse beyond

Fishing boat: anglers find a way to short-cut the walking

Commemorative boulder: the plaque is for Princess Alexandra who turned on the tap, in 1961

Someone who was trying to cut the corner emerged in unflattering colours.

Around the next corner is the Northern Wood. Perhaps, in future, privatised water companies will be inspired to name their landscaping more imaginatively, if only by immortalising their version of Cedric Brown or some other corporate hero. It is an old wood but has no separate name because it was anciently part of Clatworthy Wood – with the bit in the middle being submerged.

It brings us to the northern extremity of the reservoir, at a footbridge below the deep-cut Tripp Bottom. This is followed by the more rounded bowl of Stolford valley. The beeches of Stolford Wood are beyond.

Ford the River Tone and follow the path up through the trees. On the other side you look down on a full mile of lake before the grassy path drops down into the next belt of trees, at Syndercombe Wood. Somewhere along here, to your right, the perimeter fence apparently touches a bridleway on the outside, but there is no access to it that I could find.

If in future it is made available then there can be a diversion inland – up the hill for half a mile; turning left before Stolford; joining Syndercombe Lane in a further half mile. This and the final half mile back to the lake would give you a wider view of its setting in these southern slopes of the Brendon Hills.

Instead we shall continue our more intimate exploration, passing the 'Halfway mark'. Next is a view across to the dam, followed by Clatworthy Fishing Lodge and jetty.

On our side of the water you come to a fishing permit hut and the lake's access point from Sydercombe Lane.

The path then rounds the beautiful southern extremity of the reservoir, over the bridge below Rowes Farm and beside the big trees of Waysdown Copse. This is

the final mile and arguably the most attractive stretch of water; it usually attracts most of the fishermen but a cynic will observe that has more to do with the proximity of their cars.

Turn left after passing these, between the boathouse and fishing lodge. Then turn immediately right below its windows.

The path climbs the slope, to a gate on the skyline, and from here the power cables lead to your car.

◆

Above – The flock: Canada geese graze like a herd of flying sheep

Right – Fort wall: Clatworthy Castle is also defended by a steep slope

Ralegh's Cross and the Brendon Hills

WOODED HILLS and valleys between Williton and Dulverton looked very different in Victorian times. This otherwise pastoral landscape was dominated by Cornish-style mine workings and their engine-house chimneys above an extended cluster of more than 50 iron ore workings. They were serviced by their own railway line, the West Somerset Mineral Railway, which ran for twelve miles, across the main plateau of the Brendon Hills and then down a remarkable 1-in-4 incline on its central section, en route to Watchet Harbour, from where the rock went by sea to Newport, and thence to ironworks at Ebbw Vale.

This operated from 1856 to 1898, with a revival in 1907, and its rails were lifted during the Great War. The demise of the railway followed the decline of the industry which was blamed on imports of cheap Spanish ore which made further extraction from the Brendon Hills uneconomic.

What has been left is just one of those beam-engine exhaust chimneys, with a genuine Cornish profile as it was built by a mining engineer from Cornwall. This is the high point of our reasonably demanding **seven mile** circuit, which can be stretched to nine miles with optional diversions.

The best of these is to Beverton Pond which is the source of the River Tone. Other offerings are historic Ralegh's Cross, as the starting point, with a replica Armada-style beacon bucket. Nearby the ancient Naked Boy's Stone marks the parish boundary.

There is an amazingly deep-cut secret valley below Western Cliff Wood. More dense tree-cover extends across to Comberow railway incline and Timwood. There are woods again above Sticklepath and then a great panorama, down the vale to the Bristol Channel.

This mix of pastures and woods at the heart of the Brendon Hills straddle the eastern boundary of Exmoor National Park. As a walking experience it is much less demanding than Exmoor proper but there are still some stiff climbs, though of relative shortness, so this is a walk that can be considered by the active elderly. Expect damp patches at almost any time of year.

THE WALK ➤➤➤

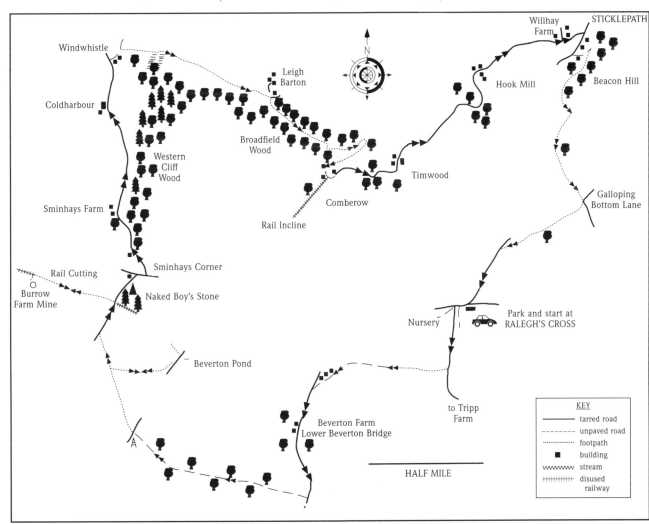

KEY
— tarred road
--- unpaved road
······ footpath
■ building
wwww stream
++++++ disused railway

HALF MILE

APPROACH RALEGH'S Cross from Exmoor or Williton, or head north-westwards from Taunton or Wiveliscombe. Park and start from Ralegh's Cross Inn, opposite the junction of the B3190 with the extension of the ridgeway towards Taunton (Ordnance Survey map reference ST 039 344).

Set off westwards, towards Brendon Hill, passing the replica Elizabethan brazier, representing one of a pair at Elworthy Barrows from before 1556 until the defeat of the Spanish Armada in 1588, and revived for the start of the Napoleonic Wars. Nearby is a conifer-shrouded 1940 pillbox and the stump of the mediaeval Ralegh's Cross.

Beverton Pond: source of the River Tone

Surviving chimney: the engine house at Burrow Farm was built in 1868

In a further 50 yards we turn left, along the second of the two tarred tracks before the nursery. This is a public bridleway to Lower Tripp Farm.

In 400 yards, at the end of the beech hedge beside the second field on the right, we turn right through a field gate, before reaching the bend in the road.

A second bridleway follows the hedge westwards across this field.

Beyond it we join a green lane and continue westwards to the barns.

Just beyond the buildings we come to a tarred lane and turn left, southwards, down to Beverton Farm and Lower Beverton Bridge.

About 400 yards beyond the bridge, around the corner on the hill, we turn right, into a double-hedged green lane. We are heading west once more.

In a mile you emerge from its beech canopy beside the radio masts above Roborough Gate Farm.

Cross the main road to the gate opposite, into Exmoor National Park, and cross the pasture diagonally, to the far corner. We are heading north-west.

A second bridleway turns right, down to the lower corner of the field, where scenic Beverton Pond

Cornish style: the engine house at Burrow Hill Mine

is the source of the River Tone. This is an optional diversion, adding a total of 1,000 yards to the walk.

From the top end of the field you join a lane and turn right, northwards, to the filled-in hump of Naked Boy's Bridge.

Here, across the stile to the left, is our next optional diversion, adding a mile, to the spectacular remains of a Cornish-style engine house, at the only surviving iron-ore workings on the Brendon Hills. We reach Burrow Farm Mine along a permissive path, following the West Somerset Mineral Railway. The mine was sunk in 1860 and reached quality ore in a thick seam at 150 feet, justifying a permanent 25-inch rotary beam engine in 1868. Its distinctive house was designed by Captain Henry Skewis, from Cornwall, and would have raised up to 200 gallons of water per minute, to prevent the mine flooding. Skips of ore were hauled up the shaft to the south of the structure, into a siding which ran

to the east. Further south is the spoil heap. The mine, including another shaft to the east, closed in 1883, due to imports of cheap Spanish ore.

Resuming our walk along the lane we pass Naked Boy's Stone, which may derive from contorted mediaeval etymology but is popularly said to have been named for the ritual whippings of Rogation Day ceremonies, to impress boundary markers as limits of safety in young minds.

Turn right and then left at the main road, to cross it at Sminhays Corner. We are heading north, towards Treborough and Roadwater.

Follow the lane, to Lower Sminhays, Coldharbour (with blocked double porches), and then Windwhistle, in a mile.

Here we turn right, beneath the power cables, and follow a track.

Just 20 yards after the gate to the barn we fork right, down into a narrow deep-cut ferny and leafy mud lane. It skirts the northern

slopes of Western Cliff Wood and Broadfield Wood, above the best secret valley of the Brendon Hills.

Proceed straight ahead, eastwards across pastures, to the farmyard at Leigh Barton, in nearly a mile.

Enter the yard but then turn right, in 25 yards, opposite the gap between the cow-stalls.

We now head south-east, through Broadfield Wood, to Comberow in half a mile.

Turn left on joining another woodland track and fork left, up the slope, in 40 yards. We are now heading north-west.

As this path approaches the end of the wood we turn sharply right and descend to the south-west, to a cottage and stream.

Proceed straight across the farmyard of Combe Row Farm and then southwards under the slanting railway bridge of the 1-in-4 incline of the central section of the mineral railway. The slope was worked by cables around large drums, using the weight of loaded trucks descending to pull empty ones back to the top, plus a small stationary engine to haul passengers – at their own risk!

After the bridge we head north-east, along the lane, to Timwood, Hook Mill, Wilhay, and Sticklepath, in a mile and a half.

Here we continue straight ahead at the first junction and then turn right at the second, southwards and upwards towards Ralegh's Cross. Pass Crown House and the Old Forge. The marker stone tells us we are five miles from Watchet.

Turn left at the next corner, above the milestone, along a track signed to Monksilver and Ralegh's Cross.

In 100 yards we turn right, steeply uphill into the wood, and proceed for a mile, southwards through field gates. Make sure you keep hedges to your left. To the right, and behind you, is a panorama on the grand scale – across to Exmoor, down to the sea at Watchet, and over the water to power station chimneys at Barry.

We come to multiple options at a bend in Galloping Bottom Lane.

Mineral railway: carried iron ore from a total of 50 mines

Boundary stone: Naked Boy's Stone near Sminhays Corner

Here we leave our field, ignore the second, and then instantly turn right into the third field (with our back to the road). Another bridleway now takes us south-westwards. Keep the banked hedge to your left and the fence to the right.

Exit through the right-hand of the two gates at the end of this strip of pasture. Then follow the next hedge, also keeping it to your left.

Turn left on reaching the B3190 and return to the top of the hill at Ralegh's Cross. ◆

Luxborough and Churchtown

Saddle-back: distinctive roof on St Mary's tower at Churchtown

A BIG PARISH of 4,728 acres at the heart of the wooded Brendon Hills, Luxborough rises to 1,289 feet with the most easterly proper peak of Exmoor National Park. This is amid the cairns of scrubby Withycombe Common.

Superficially, the landscape is dominated by Forestry Commission and Crown Estate pines, but our walk avoids much of the oppressive sameness of modern times by searching out characterful vestiges of its ancient track system. Perley Way is a gem, floristically and visually, with the bonus that for the third walk in succession I dropped one of my Ball Pentel Fine Point pens (why I always carry two) which perhaps still awaits an eagle-eyed walker. I mention the

tradename in the hope that magazine publishers Stephen Pugsley and Roy Smart will find sponsors for my litter as an ongoing promotion. I'll revert to Biro or some other brand if they acquire a free supply from another maker. The lost pen eluded route-tester

Tony Poyntz-Wright, whose direction suggestions have been incorporated in the text. For the triple test a copy was submitted to Bill Gurnett who is Head Ranger of the National Park.

As for the pre-forestation landscape, Luxborough's deep-cut

Village centre: the Royal Oak at Luxborough

valleys are much as county historian John Collinson described them in 1791. Fifty buildings, half of them small farms, with 'the rest mostly mean mud-walled cottages, covered with thatch' – requiring deletion of 'mean', perhaps, but it is a sharper word than a patronising 'nice'.

Non-farms and cottages have included the Luxborough Arms, formerly in the hamlet of Churchtown, and the Royal Oak, still in leafy Kingsbridge. That's now replaced Churchtown as the Luxborough village of Luxborough parish, and has even boasted a post office. Use it or lose it; I was one of the last customers, but only for a can of Coke.

Churchtown retains the parish church, which is St Mary's of stout tower with distinctive slate-gabled topping. This saddle-back roof dates from the 1891 restoration but perpetuates a feature dating back several centuries. Lower parts of the tower are 15th century and the chancel buttress and windows have been dated to 1230.

There is also an ancient churchyard cross and a couple of stone table-tombs. The earliest documentary mention of the church is its inclusion in a gift of property to the new Bruton Priory at its foundation in the 12th century.

Stained glass includes a colourful reflection of empire, with a window provided by Charles Lethbridge in memory of a son killed in the Boer War siege of Ladysmith, in 1900.

An old trades directory, from that time, refers to 'much uncultivated land' around Luxborough. There are still pockets of what used to be termed 'marginal land' – otherwise transferred by agricultural subsidies, or afforested – and what remains we shall search out, in this **five mile** exploration of the north-east corner of the parish. The walk is suitable for the active elderly but there are steepish slopes and a couple of instances of rough ground. Other parts are liable to be boggy.

THE WALK ➤➤➤

CROSS THE Brendon Hills along the B3224, and turn north to Luxborough, midway between Heath Poult Cross in the west and Brendon Hill Chapel on the approach from Ralegh's Cross. Drive down into Luxborough and park and start from the car park opposite the village hall, in the part of the parish called Kingsbridge on the map but Luxborough on the ground (Ordnance Survey map reference SS 984 376).

The contributions box is in the north-east corner and we begin our walk from here by turning left and walking into the centre of the village.

Turn left at the junction, opposite the elegant thatch of Rambler Cottage, and cross the stream. Pass the Royal Oak of Luxborough.

Then turn left, beside the lower stone wall of the garden of Millmead, which you keep to your right. Take care following the public footpath along what at the time of writing is an overgrown adverse slope.

Beyond the gardens we cross a stile into a pasture and follow the stream, keeping it and the hillside wood to our left. We are heading west.

In 200 yards you turn left, over a stile, and cross the stream at a footbridge. On the other side we join a woodland path and turn right along it, still heading west.

Pass East Thorney Cottage, in the middle of Church Wood, which

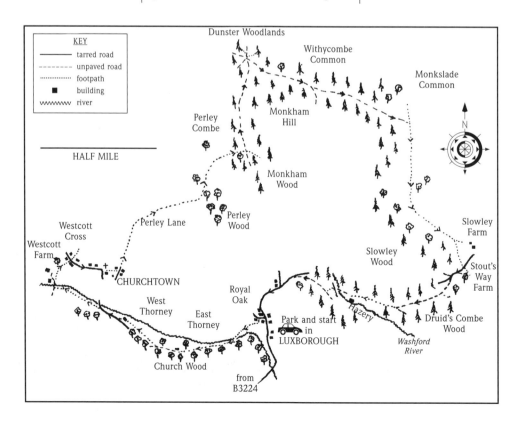

must have been named for past ownership rather than an actual building.

Fork right 75 yards beyond the cottage, keeping the stream in sight – down the slope to our right.

Beyond West Thorney Cottage the path continues straight ahead up the rise and joins the tarred road. Turn right along it, down towards Churchtown, but only as far as the bridge, in 225 yards.

Turn left immediately before the bridge, through the field gate, and walk straight ahead. Keep the stream to your right.

Cross the stile in the hedgerow and follow the stream to the gate on the other side of this pasture.

Turn right and cross the stream, beside the ford, and approach Westcott Farm. We are heading north.

At the bend there are a number of options and ours is the lesser one, being a bridleway gate facing you straight ahead, between elder bushes and a tangle of Japanese knotweed. Beyond this gate the track becomes a deep-cut hollow way which climbs north-eastwards, into Churchtown. We emerge into the light beside West Cott Cross Cottages (signed with an aberrant

Top – Perley Lane: between banks of rose-bay willow herb

Right – Bygone sculpture: holly-smothered plough beside Slowley Wood

Informal parking: set-aside agriculture at Slowley Farm

apostrophe, to continue the alliteration).

Turn right, downhill, to Battels bungalow, from where we proceed straight ahead, eastwards through the churchyard. Note the red sandstone shaft of its mediaeval preaching cross.

On the other side we pass Church Cottage.

Now turn left, up Perley Lane. In 25 yards this becomes a double-hedged green lane. Walk the length of it, uphill to the oaks of Perley Wood in a kilometre, to the north-east.

On reaching the trees we continue straight ahead, through the gate, to keep the woodland fence to our right and descend northwards into a dip below the pine forest.

Here we pass the footings of ruined Perley Barn. Cross the stream and go straight ahead through the gate, eastwards into Monkham Hill Plantation.

In 200 yards we come to a woodland crossroads and turn left, uphill and northwards. Keep going straight ahead until you reach the Dunster Woodland forest road at the top, at a 6-way junction of tracks. We are now 1,250 feet above sea level with a view northwards to the Bristol Channel and South Wales.

Turn right, south-eastwards, with the pines of Monkham Hill to the right and scrub of Withycombe Common to the left.

In 500 yards we continue straight ahead, ignoring a wider turning to the right. Then in a further 700 yards we come to the edge of the woods and a panorama of the Somerset coast and Quantock Hills. Carhampton is the village down to the left, with Steep Holm being the offshore island.

Approach a field gate in the corner but do not go through it. Our bridleway crosses another and we turn right to join it, through a second gate which is set in the embanked hedge.

We are now heading south, straight across a big field, to a gate to the right of the taller stone-walled beech hedge.

In the next pasture the track follows the hedge southwards, to the rim of the valley, and then swings leftwards, south-east, to descend into it. Pass a holly bush currently sculpting an abandoned plough.

Fork right on approaching Slowley Farm.

Turn right along Stout's Way Lane, south-westwards through the woods.

In 150 yards, at the wide Forest Enterprise parking bays, we bear left from the tarred road, down a stony track into the conifers of Slowley Wood.

Ignore turnings and continue straight ahead, south-west. Leave the main track as it turns sharply

Wooded hills: from Perley Wood, across Monkham Wood, with the eastern Brendons beyond

left, 500 yards from the road, and continue straight ahead along a grassy path. This joins a driveway at Hazery which we follow to a bridge over the Washford River.

Then cross the tarred road to a permissive path on the other side. It climbs the hillside and becomes awkwardly steep in about 90 yards.

Here we join a forest road and turn right along it, to head north-west, through Birchen Wood.

Turn left on rejoining the valley road, after passing above a disused quarry, and follow it straight ahead at the junction, to return to Luxborough around the next corner. ◆

Druid's Combe: typical of the valley farms surrounded by pines

Dunster Castle and Park

STARTING A walk from the most beautiful town in Britain throws up an immediate problem. It is neither people nor parking. The latter is provided for and the former pleasant, with the positive advantage that they bring life and facilities on a scale that would not otherwise grace the fringe economy of Exmoor's north-east corner.

Dunster is Dunster Castle plus an endless collection of additional ruins, relics and buildings that are worth a second glance if not a photograph as well.

The idea of this **four mile** walk is to see Dunster Castle and then put it into the context of the landscape with an easy exploration of the hills and woods to the south. Where the problem starts is that it is impossible to do that without also being distracted sideways and upwards by an innumerable assortment of other goodies.

Dunster deserves a full day. Before visiting the castle and embarking on the walk you need to 'do' the town – and that can take hours!

All but the obvious things are beyond the scope of an article and how much of my writing you will be able to read is going to be dependent upon the editing process.

For starters there is the distinctive oddity of the Yarn Market, at the wider end of the High Street, which is in the care of English Heritage. Built in 1589 it was used for the sale of 'Dunsters' – lengths of fine woollen cloth for men's suits.

Its 'GL 1647' weathervane is for George Luttrell who had it repaired after it was ripped apart by Civil War cannon balls during the siege of Dunster Castle. Cannon-fire left a splintered hole in one of the huge oak rafters.

The Butter Cross, a 15th-century wayside cross that is now reduced to a stump and plinth, has been moved to the far end of St George's Street, where it can also be reached by a path from Priory Green. It originally stood at the junction of the High Street and Church Street. 'By the traffic lights,' I was told, which sounds a non sequitur.

Above its present location, in the trees, is Conygar Tower. This was erected by Henry Fownes Luttrell in 1775 as a navigation aid and 'a prospect tower'. Its two tall four-windowed storeys must have provided the perfect view of a perfect place. It is one of the finest positioned Somerset follies.

Down among the plentiful quaintness of the town itself is another circular stone tower which is also among the best of the 25 of its kind that have survived in the county. The Dovecote at Priory

Castle Tor: the tree-clad hill that was surmounted by the great keep of Dunster Castle

Green was a monastic pigeon-house. Built in the 13th or 14th century, it has a conical roof that is surmounted by a bird-table and weathervane, above the 'glover' which is the circular opening for the doves to enter the building. Inside it is complete with nesting holes and the revolving axle of the 'potence' and platform from which eggs and young birds were harvested. The little building was excellently restored in 1989.

Likewise, that decade, the Priory Gardens which were bought by the people of Dunster in 1980. Buildings of the Old Priory, which housed the Prior and three Benedictine cannons, are on the north side of St George's Church. It was dissolved in 1536 and the gardens were bought by Lady Margaret Luttrell in 1543, for £85. They became the walled kitchen gardens for the castle.

St George's was a Priory Church, from 1090, and incorporates Norman work. It is also the resting place of the Luttrells and their vandalised effigies, plus numerous monuments to the family that owned and occupied Dunster Castle from 1375 and for the next

600 years, until the death of Mrs Alys Luttrell in 1974.

Lieutenant-Colonel G. W. F. Luttrell gave the castle, with 48 acres of grounds and the 18th-century Castle Mill, to the National Trust. The watermill is now back in working order and can be visited in the course of the walk.

Lastly, before moving on from the town to the castle, admire the High House in Church Street which has become known as the Old Nunnery. There was never a nunnery in Dunster but the building was given by Sir Hugh

Giant's causeway: piles of outgoing timber, in Dunster Park

Pero to the Abbess of Cleeve in 1346. It has projecting gables and 'fish-scale' wall tiling that clads the second and third storeys.

The present Dunster Castle dates from 1070 when William de Mohun built his fortress, a bit of which survives in the northern bastion and curtain wall.

A Latin inscription over the fireplace of the later Great Hall records, however, that there was an earlier castle, on the wooded knoll that is the site of the keep: 'Here on this Tor, Aluric the Saxon had his Castle in the reign of Edward the Confessor.'

William's successors, Sir Reynold de Mohun and the first Baron Mohun, beefed up the battlements and added towers and the gatehouse, in 1220. It survives in its 15th-century state.

What would have been the great landmark of Exmoor, the keep on the Tor, was rebuilt from Aluric's timber castle. Its Norman replacement was followed in the 12th century by a great tower of stone. It was strong, vast, and square.

That would still stand but for an accident of history which saw it on the wrong side, being held by Royalists, in the Civil War. Six months of siege brought them to starvation and surrender. Cromwell then ordered demolition, which was carried out by 300 men.

The flat fields below the castle were then its moat, being inundated by the sea until the 18th century, when they were drained for The Lawns polo ground. Indeed there must still have been an arm of the sea running up to the walls of Dunster Castle in 1645 because the Royalists attempted to break the siege with a man-of-war. It went aground at low tide and was captured by a squadron of Parliamentary cavalry.

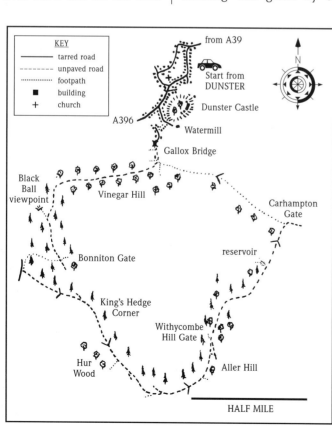

The Great Hall is Elizabethan, dating from 1580, and was commissioned by George Luttrell. Work continued until 1620. It was partially rebuilt and extended, with a new portico, by Anthony Salvin in 1869.

Outside, on the terrace, oranges and lemons have been growing beside the south wall since before 1700. Sub-tropical plants survive and even flourish in the microclimate of battlements near the sea.

THE WALK ➤➤➤

WALK SOUTHWARDS through the town and turn left from the A396 between Woodville House and Millstream Cottage (Ordnance Survey map reference SS 990 434). This is Mill Lane, which is signed to 'Dunster Working Mill' and as 'Footpath to Pack Horse Bridge'. To the left you pass an Ebenezer Chapel of 1811 which also has a stone for a Wesleyan day school of 1825, and was rebuilt in 1855.

In 150 yards you have the option of continuing to see the watermill but our walk turns right, following the 'Pack Horse Bridge' path beside Millhaven.

Turn right in Park Street, where you are treated to thatch and

flowers at Old Stream Cottage and Rose Cottage opposite.

The public road ends in a ford at the River Avill, which we cross by the mediaeval Gallox Bridge. It is an ancient monument in the care of English Heritage. The double arches of the bridge seem to have concentrated the flow and gouged out the ford which is immediately downstream.

Continue straight ahead on the other side, passing thatched

cottages 28 and 30. Above them is a crossroads of tracks, where we again continue ahead. This path is signed 'Timberscombe, Luxborough, via Croydon Hill'.

It climbs uphill through the ferny woods on the side of Gallox Hill. In 150 yards, to your right and down the slope in the holly bushes, is Gallox Well, not that I spotted it.

At the summit of Vinegar Hill the main track bends to the left, but it is worth turning right for 70

Gallox Bridge: mediaeval packhorse bridge beside a ford

Outward bound: the path to the hills exits Dunster beside an expanse of thatch

yards, to find a viewpoint seat above Avill Farm, where you look from rhododendron-covered slopes into the heart of Exmoor.

The main track continues around Black Ball, with blue marker posts and Crown Estate arrows '2' and '3'. Next, at Bonnington Gate, the blue-marked track continues uphill, but here we leave it.

Instead you turn right, following '2' and '3' downhill. In the valley you drop down virtually to the tarred road but do not join it.

Now turn left, along the unmade road that follows the stream and is signed 'Public Path Carhampton'. It runs along the foot of King's Hedge Coppice.

In half a mile we continue straight ahead, ignoring the left turn that is signposted to Dunster. In a further quarter of a mile you pass a footbridge, without crossing it, and again continue straight ahead.

The woodland road is now taking us uphill. Ignore the blue-marked path which forks down to the right. Yours is uphill, for half a mile.

You'll see arrows '2' and '3' twice more, but ignore them the second time where another track joins from the left.

At the top you come to Withycombe Hill Gate, beside a junction of tracks.

Continue straight ahead, keeping on the main track towards Carhampton. The ancient stone wall to your left is shared by foxgloves and mature beech trees. It encloses the mediaeval Dunster Park which has been partially re-forested, though it still has expanses of bracken moorland and clusters of old oaks. The main plantations are to your left, and then fields to the right.

Half a mile after Withycombe Hill Gate we leave the trees and pass a reservoir, which is on our left. In 300 yards the main track turns to the right.

Here you turn left, through Carhampton Gate, to enter Dunster Park and head towards Dunster Castle. In the dip the path crosses two small streams.

From the semi-wooded slope beyond the next rise you have one of the best views of the castle – magical in sultry summer heat – which is now to your right.

The path descends to a gate and stile in the trees. On the other side we turn left and then right, to retrace our steps across Gallox Bridge and into Dunster.

Someone there must have a sense of humour – the church chimes played *There's no place like home* as I re-entered town.

It was that time of day, so perhaps they were telling the tourist hordes to go. The barrier had already dropped on the National Trust car park. ◆

Index